Mastering English Usage

ROBERT ILSON
JANET WHITCUT

PHOENIX
ELT

incorporating
PRENTICE HALL MACMILLAN

New York   London   Toronto   Sydney   Tokyo   Singapore

Published 1995 by
Phoenix ELT
Campus 400, Maylands Avenue
Hemel Hempstead
Hertfordshire HP2 7EZ
A division of
Prentice Hall International (UK) Ltd
First published 1994 by
Prentice Hall International (UK) Ltd

Typeset in 10/12 pt Palatino by
Fakenham Photosetting Ltd, Fakenham, Norfolk

Printed and bound in Great Britain by
Redwood Books, Trowbridge, Wiltshire

Library of Congress Cataloging-in-Publication Data

Whitcut, Janet.
Mastering English usage / Janet Whitcut, Robert Ilson.
    p.   cm.
1. English language – Textbooks for foreign speakers.
2. English language – Usage. I. Ilson, Robert. II. Title.
PE1128.W716   1994
428.2′4 – dc20   93–41825

British Library Cataloguing in Publication Data

A catalogue record for this book is available from the
British Library

ISBN 0–13–554171–9

2   3   4   5   98   97   96   95

Acknowledgments

Our general approach to the English language is as close as we can make it to that of *A Comprehensive Grammar of the English Language* (Longman: 1985) and 'The Survey of English Usage' (University College London).

We are grateful to our students, our teachers, and our colleagues. Among those who have helped us most are: Professor Morton Benson, Dr John Kahn, Professor Igor Mel'čuk, Professor Toshihiro Ogura, Dr Alois Ringhofer, Dr Shigeto Yawata. To the late Professor Dwight Bolinger, whose dictum 'Every Difference Makes A Difference' has so often inspired us to tease out subtle nuances of meaning and use, we owe a debt that can never be repaid. We hope that we shall be of as much help to you as these good friends have been to us.

Robert Ilson, Janet Whitcut

Robert Ilson (American) is an Honorary Research Fellow of University College London and the Editor of the *International Journal of Lexicography*.

Janet Whitcut (British) is the author of many books and articles on English Usage for both learners and native speakers.

Introduction

Why?

You already know English well enough to read a book in it, but you want to know English even better. It is the purpose of our book to help you to do so. You have a problem. You look it up here. You find a solution to the problem, and use the solution yourself. Your knowledge of English has increased. The help provided by our book is the kind of help we would like to have when we learn a foreign language ourselves.

On the other hand, why bother? Everybody makes mistakes now and then. Most of the time you manage to get your meaning across, so why make the extra effort to learn what is in our book? There are several reasons why this effort is worth making.

(1) Some mistakes are obviously wrong. If you make an obvious mistake, people will try to understand you, but that means more work for them. It is better manners for you to make the effort to get something right than to oblige other people to make the effort to interpret something wrong. Such a mistake is *I am student* instead of *I am a student* (see **a and the (2)**).

(2) Some mistakes are not obviously wrong, and they are even worse. People will assume they know what you mean. They will be misled. The consequences can be serious. It is such a mistake to say *You mustn't come to my party* (a prohibition) when you mean *You don't have to come to my party* (a choice) (see **must (1b)**).

(3) More generally, your USE of English and your UNDERSTANDING of English are connected. The closer your English comes to that of native speakers, the more easily and accurately you will understand them. The better you understand native speakers, the easier it will be for you to remember what THEY say and write as models for what YOU say and write. Better use makes for better understanding. Better understanding makes for better use.

But won't all the information in our book worry you so much that you will hesitate to use English at all? Won't your effort to increase the ACCURACY of your English diminish its FLUENCY? We certainly hope not! The first few times you express yourself in a new way it may feel a little strange. But after a while the new way will become familiar to you. Besides, it will be reinforced by the English you hear and see. Soon you will use the new way even more freely than you used the old. You may even forget the old way altogether – and forget where you learned about the new one! Once you have mastered the solution to a problem through our book, you won't need to look the problem up again. Your self-confidence will grow, and with it your freedom from the fear of using English.

What?

The problems solved in this book are chiefly of grammar (e.g. **comparatives; conditionals; countable and uncountable nouns**), vocabulary (e.g. **border/frontier/boundary; feminine forms; word and preposition**), and communicative function (e.g. **apologies; asking for things; complaining; invitations**). But other types of problem are also considered (e.g. **commas; hyphens;** (formats for) **letters**). The analysis of some problems includes a discussion of pronunciation and intonation.

These problems have been chosen for any or all of three reasons:
(a) they are frequent among learners of English whose own languages are very different from one another;
(b) they are difficult not only because of the way English differs from other languages but also because of the structure of English itself;
(c) they are serious because they can cause misunderstanding or embarrassment.

Our book is written in 'the British English of the 1990s' (see **American and British English**). But we give so much information about American English, too, that our book will be of use to students of either variety.

How?

Examples

The 'typical mistakes' and 'typical problems' are accompanied by one or more examples, either taken or adapted from those we have encountered as English teachers or those we have been asked about by students or colleagues. The examples of both correct and incorrect usage are often made up by us to clarify the problem, but are sometimes taken directly from authentic British and American sources, old and new: in such cases the sources are identified. In the course of our discussion of them, the 'typical mistakes' are all corrected, the 'typical problems' all solved.

Conventions

We have tried to avoid unusual conventions of presentation, but have used the following to save space:

AmE: 'American English'.

BrE: 'British English'.

esp.: 'especially'.

* (as in *I am student*) precedes something wrong.

? (as in *?I wish I had such a car*) precedes something you should probably not use yourself.

/ (as in *and/or*) separates alternatives.

/ / enclose pronunciations.

( ) enclose comments such as 'informal' or 'BrE', optional elements as in *a(n)*, identification of sources as in (Shakespeare), many cross-references, and glosses (= short explanations like this one). Comments such as (BrE) or (informal) apply usually to what follows them, but sometimes to what precedes: *an old car*/(BrE slang) *banger*; *a lift* (BrE)/(AmE) *elevator*; *gaol* (BrE)/*jail*.

The use of / and ( ) makes clear the scope of these comments.

Intonation Symbols

'	'stressed syllable'
⌣	'fall'
⌣	'rise'
V	'fall-rise'
∧	'rise-fall'

Pronunciation Symbols

Consonants		Vowels	
/b/	bed	/iː/	sheep
/d/	dog	/ɪ/	ship
/f/	fish	/e/	ten
/g/	garden	/æ/	man
/h/	hat	/ɒ/	clock
/k/	key	/ɔː/	talk
/l/	leg	/ɑː/	half
/m/	mountain	/ʊ/	book
/n/	needle	/uː/	food
/p/	pen	/ʌ/	cup
/r/	red	/ɜː/	girl
/s/	sun	/ə/	about
/t/	tea	/eɪ/	tail
/v/	verb	/əʊ/	phone
/w/	watch	/aɪ/	like
/j/	yellow	/aʊ/	house
/z/	zoo	/ɔɪ/	boy
/θ/	birthday	/ɪə/	here
/tʃ/	chair	/eə/	there
/dʒ/	jam		
/ð/	mother		
/ŋ/	sing		
/ʃ/	shoe		
/ʒ/	television		

a and the

1. a or an?

It depends on pronunciation, not on spelling. Use *an* before words, letters or symbols that begin with a vowel sound: *an apple, an 'S'*, but *a £5 note*. The combination *eu* is pronounced with a 'y' sound, so it should be *a European*. The letter *u* at the beginning of a word may also have this sound, or it may not; so it should be *a unit, a useful book*, but *an umbrella*. The letter *o* may, or may not, be pronounced with a 'w' sound, so it should be *an orange* but *a one-legged man*. With groups of initials, use *an* before A, E, F, H, I, L, M, N, O, R, S, X: *an H-bomb, an RAF officer*, but *a BBC announcer*. Before acronyms, it also depends on the pronunciation: *a NATO ('neɪtəʊ) officer*, but *shaped like an N*.

Initial *h* in a stressed syllable takes *a* if the *h* is pronounced; *a 'hair, a 'hero, a 'history, a 'hologram, a 'hyste 'rectomy*. If the *h* is not pronounced, it takes *an*: *an heir, an hour, an 'honour, an 'hono 'rarium*. It is not wrong, though perhaps old-fashioned, to use *an* before an unstressed but pronounced *h*: *a(n) ho'tel, a(n) his'torian*.

2. a(n) or nothing at all?

Use *a, an* before singular countable nouns: *I'm a pensioner; I'm an MP*. (But see 5 below.) Before names, *a(n)* can mean 'a painting, drawing, etc., by': *a Turner*. (See also **countable and uncountable nouns**, and **verb or noun**?)

3. a or one?

It often does not matter. You can say *There's a* (or *one*) *parking space left*, or order *a* (or *one*) *beer and two coffees*, wait for *an* (or *one*) *hour*, or spend *a* (or *one*) *hundred dollars*. But *one* is a number, part of the counting system, in contrast with *two, three*. Use *one* when you are talking about numbers. Compare:

> *One student failed the exam, but all the rest passed.*
> *If a student fails the exam, he or she can try again.*

4. a or the?

It often does not matter. You can say *Thanks for a* (or *the*) *lovely evening*, or *We set ourselves a* (or *the*) *target of £500*, or *A* (or *The*) *cat is a land animal* (but *Man is a land animal*). But use *the* when the noun has already been used with the same meaning. Compare:

> *She wore a jacket and a sweater. The sweater* (= that same sweater) *was pink.*
> *She wore a jacket and a sweater. A sweater keeps* (or *Sweaters keep*) *you warm.*
> (The second sentence makes a general statement about sweaters, not just *her* sweater.)

Use *the* when it is clear which one you mean: *I'm going to the post office* (= the one near here).

Use *the* when the words after the noun explain which one you mean: *the University of London; the man you met yesterday.* (But *A man you meet by chance may become your husband.* This is not about a particular man.)

Use *the* when there is only one: *the moon; the year 1992.*

5. the or nothing at all?

> TYPICAL MISTAKES: **The patience is a virtue. *He works at the night. *We crossed Atlantic.*

With certain words, use *the* only where something else tells us what kind or which one is meant. This is true of abstract nouns, such as *beauty, defence, light, sound, work, transport, time, music: Henry dislikes administration. The administration of the department keeps him busy.*

It is also true of names of materials, such as *wine, silk, coal*, and of meals, such as *lunch.*

It is also true of plurals used in a general sense: *They play quartets. They play the quartets of Beethoven* (or *Beethoven's quartets*). Some other words are used without *the.* Omit *the* before words for sports and illnesses: *She enjoys tennis. She's got flu.*

Omit *the* before *school, hospital* (BrE), *church, bed, college, prison* and (increasingly, esp. in BrE) *university*, when speaking not of the place but of the function. Compare:

> *She went to hospital; she's in hospital* (this means, as a patient).
> *I went to the hospital to see her* (this means, as a visitor, but AmE has *the hospital* in all these cases).

You cannot always do this. People who work in an office *go to the office*, or are *at the office*; and you go *to the bank* to get money and *to the market* to shop.

Omit *the* before means of transport or communication, after *by: by car, by train, by plane, by sea* (= in a ship), *by telephone, by radio.* (But *by/on the four o'clock train* tells us which train is meant. See **transport**.)

Omit *the* when *man, woman* are used as singular nouns in a general sense: *Man is a land animal* (compare **4** above).

Omit *the* when people are directly addressed: *Good morning, General!*

The is usually omitted before offices and positions of which there is only one, after verbs such as *elect, appoint, become,* and after *of* and *as*:

They elected him President (there is only one President).
As (the) head teacher, she is responsible for the timetable.
Stephen became king in AD 1135 (compare **2** above).

Names either include *the*, or do not. Names that include *the* are:

plural names	*the Smiths, the Philippines*
seas	*the Atlantic, the Mediterranean*
rivers	*the Ganges, the Nile*
mountain ranges	*the Alps, the Andes*
groups of islands	*the Galapagos, the Dodecanese*
some bays and gulfs	*the Bay of Biscay, the Persian Gulf* (but *Botany Bay, Hudson's Bay*)
deserts	*the Sahara, the Kalahari*
countries whose name includes an adjective, or is a phrase	*the United States, the CIS, the People's Republic of China*
ships, hotels, newspapers, cinemas, and theatres	*the QEII, the Beagle, the Ritz, The Times, the Colosseum*

Names without *the* are:

names of people	*Mary, Mr Butcher*
days and months	*Tuesday, November*
festivals and religions	*Easter, Islam*
towns	*Paris, Delhi* (exception: *The Hague*)
continents, and most countries	*Europe, Iran* (*the* is now commonly omitted, particularly in AmE, in *(the) Lebanon, (the) Sudan, (the) Gambia, (the) Ukraine*)
most lakes, islands, and mountains	*Windermere, Crete, Everest* (mountains with *the*, such as *the Matterhorn*, are those with German names)
stars and planets	*Sirius, Mercury*
features in towns	*Heathrow* (= London Airport), *Central Park* (= in New York)

Like *42nd Street* and *Delancey Street, London Road* would be the name of a road where people live and work, whereas *the London road* is simply the one that leads to London. (See **street**.) Note that a name such as *French*, without *the*, means the language, but *the French* means the French people. Compare:

He can't speak French.
The French produce good wine.
(See **nationality**.)

Some ordinary words can be used as names, and are then without *the*:

The mother of these children.
Let's ask Mother!

Some names can be used like ordinary words, and then include *the*:

Christmas is a winter festival.
The Christmas when we went skiing.

6. the or my, his, her?

In certain idioms, one must use *the*: *He hit the girl on the* (not *her*) *head*. Here, it is clear whose head we are talking about! But say *My* (not **The*) *toe is hurting*, or someone might ask 'Whose toe?'

7. the . . . the . . .

It is normal to use a pair of *the*s with comparatives: *the sooner the better*. Do not use *that* in these clauses: *the faster* (**that*) *she works, the more mistakes* (**that*) *she makes*. It is not wrong, but old-fashioned, to use inversion after the second *the* here: *the more people who go, the cheaper will be the fare*.

abide see stand

about

1. | TYPICAL MISTAKE: **She was an about twelve-year-old girl.*

About, approximately, roughly and (esp. in AmE) *around* can all be used with numbers and measurements: *It costs about £5*. These words cannot be used as in the 'typical mistake' above. Write instead: *She was about 12 years old*, or *She was a girl of about 12*.

2. about/on

They can both mean 'on the subject of', but *on* is for more serious contexts. Compare:

a story about two rabbits
a lecture on hydrocarbons.
(For *about to*, see **future tense(2)**.)

above

1. above/over

They are often used in the same way: *There was a mirror above/over the fireplace.*

When the meaning is 'higher than something', or 'from side to side of something', use *above*: *He raised both hands above his head. The dog jumped over the gate.* To give the idea of covering and protection, use *over*: *He spread a blanket over the sleeping child.* (See also **under**.)

2. | TYPICAL MISTAKE: **Discuss the quotation from above.*

Above and *below* are used to refer to what comes earlier, or later, in a piece of writing. You can speak of *the above quotation* or *the quotation above*, but do not use *from* except in such phrases as *From the above (quotation) we learn . . . .* Note that *the quotation below* is possible, but not **the below quotation* or **the below*.

accommodation, -ache see countable and uncountable nouns

actual see false friends

addressing people

When you want to attract the attention of a stranger, it is usual to begin by saying *Excuse me!* In BrE, it is rather formal to say *Sir* or *Madam*, though these are used more freely in AmE. *Ma'am* /mæm/ is short for *Madam*. You will hear these words in shops and restaurants: *Is this the right colour, Madam? Are you ready to order now, sir?*

Some, but not all, words for occupations can be used in direct address. These include *Doctor, Nurse, Professor, Waiter, Waitress, Driver, Operator* (on the telephone), and all the military and naval ranks such as *Admiral, Sergeant* (but not **Teacher!* Call your teacher *Miss* or *Sir*, or use the name). *Taxi!* can be used to hail one.

At the beginning of a formal speech, people usually say (*My Lords,*) *Ladies and Gentlemen.*

If you know someone's name, of course you can call them by it; and the use of the first name alone is now much more common than it was. If you do not know them well enough to say simply *Susan* or *Peter*, say *Mr Brown, Mrs Ross*, etc. *Mr, Mrs, Ms* are not usually used alone. Add the name.

You address grandparents, aunts and uncles as *grannie, grandma, granddad, grandpa, auntie* (or *Aunt Jane* or *Auntie Jane*), and *uncle* (or *Uncle Bill*). (For what to call your parents, see **father**.)

Finally, there are many ways to address people for whom you feel love or friendship, such as *darling, love, honey* (esp. AmE), and many more if you want to be nasty, such as *stupid*. The learner should be careful in using these more emotional words, since their appropriateness depends on social position, level of formality, and the sex of the speaker and hearer.

adjective or adverb?

1. Many adjectives are used, rather than their related *-ly* adverbs, to show the 'result' of a verb. You can say *Screw the lid down tight*, which means 'so that it is tight'.

 After the verbs *look, sound, taste, smell* and *feel* when they describe the effect something has on your senses, use an adjective: *The dog looked hungry* (compare *It looked hungrily at the steak*). The test is whether the verb could be replaced by *be*: the dog *was* hungry.

2. feel

This verb is a special case. We use an adjective after it to show what someone feels: *I feel sick.* We use an adverb to show how someone feels about something: *I felt differently about it.* If you *feel bad*, either you are ill or you have a bad conscience, but in the latter case *badly* is also correct: *I felt very bad(ly) about what happened.* If you *feel good* you are happy, but if you *feel well* you are healthy.

3. bad(ly)

Badly and *well*, not *bad* and *good*, are the right choice when we speak of the way in which a verb is 'done': *She drives well/badly.*

4. right, wrong

Right has many uses as an adverb: *Turn right. I'll come right home.* In the senses 'correctly, incorrectly', *right* and *wrong* have the alternative forms *rightly* and *wrongly*. In short constructions, prefer *right, wrong* after the verb, *rightly* or *wrongly* before it: *He guessed right. They spell it wrong.*

 In longer and more complex sentences, you may prefer the slightly more formal *rightly, wrongly*: *You must have been wrongly informed. Rightly* and *wrongly* can also mean 'justly, unjustly', rather than 'in a right/wrong way': *He was wrongly accused of the theft* (or *Wrongly, he was accused . . .*).

5. quick, slow

These can be used as adverbs, and are rather less formal than *quickly, slowly*: *Come quick!* (or *quickly*). *Eat slower* (or *more slowly*). Prefer *quick, quicker* for the sense 'in a short(er) time, soon(er)': *You'll get there quicker by air.*

 You can avoid the choice between *quick* and *quickly* by using *fast*, especially for anything to do with vehicles. *Fast* can be an adjective (*a fast car*) or an adverb (*drive even faster*).

6. loud

This is correct as an adverb, though less formal than *loudly*: *Don't shout so loud* (or *loudly*). *Speak louder* (or *more loudly*). Prefer *loudly* for the idea of insistent, rowdy voices: *He called loudly for help.*

afterwards/after (that)/later

1. after

> TYPICAL MISTAKES: *We'll come after ten minutes. *The office is open after 9.30.

When you mean 'after the end of', say *in ten minutes*, or (esp. BrE) *in ten minutes' time*; and say *from 9.30* if you are stating the normal opening hours. Say *after 9.30* only when expressing surprise at the lateness of an evening closing time: *Will the office still be open after 9.30?*

2. afterwards (AmE also *afterward*) and *after that* both mean 'after some earlier event' or 'then': *I'm working till six, but I'll see you afterwards/after that.* In addition, *after that* can mean 'because of that': *He was caught stealing. After that, of course, we had to sack him.*
    Later simply means 'at a later time': *I'll tell you later* (= not now).

3. after/afterwards

> TYPICAL MISTAKE: *They arrived after.

After can be used like *afterwards*, but except in informal English it needs another time adverb: *They arrived soon/shortly after.*

ago

> TYPICAL MISTAKE: *It is 20 years ago since he left.

Use *ago* with verbs in the simple past tense, and do not combine it with *since*: *It was 20 years ago that he left.* (See **since**.)

agree

> TYPICAL MISTAKE: *Do you agree with these terms?

One *agrees to* terms and conditions and demands and proposals, which means 'accept, give consent to' them. One *agrees with* a person if one shares their opinion: *Do you agree with her?* Thus, one might *agree to* a policy without liking it. You will hear people saying things like *I don't agree with* (= approve of) *capital punishment*, but it is better to use *approve of*, or *hold with*, here.
    People *agree about* something if they share the same opinion of it. They *agree in* something if they start out with the same point of view about it: *We found that we agreed in our estimate of him.* People *agree on/upon* something if after discussion they reach a decision: *We agreed on a suitable site for the new building.*

aim/goal/objective/target

They can all mean much the same thing: something that one hopes to attain. On the whole, one *achieves* an *aim* (or a *goal*, or an *objective*) when speaking of less measurable things: *He achieved his aim of qualifying as a surgeon.* One *reaches* a *target* when speaking of measurable things, such as money and numbers: *We reached this year's production target of 50,000 dishwashers.*

air

> TYPICAL MISTAKES: *The air blew the tree down. *Open the window to let in the open air.

Moving air is *wind*, so it was the *wind* that *blew the tree down.* You are in the *open air* when you are outside, out of doors; but it is *fresh* (= pure, cool) *air* that comes in when you *open a window.*

all/the whole (of the)/the entire

1. > TYPICAL MISTAKES: *The whole students were present. *She drank the whole milk.

The adjectives *whole* and *entire* are used with singular countable nouns. You can say: *He spent the entire morning in bed. The whole city was burning.* Note also the common combinations *the whole time, the whole way, the whole truth.*

   Whole and *entire* can be used with plurals, to say that something is complete, and not just a part: *Whole forests and entire rivers may disappear.*

   All is followed by *of* before pronouns, and often before the determiners *the, this, my,* and so on: 'Your letter gave pleasure to all of us' (Jane Austen, 1813) (or *Your letter gave pleasure to us all*). It is common in AmE, but less so in BrE, to use *all of* before plural nouns: *All (of) the students were present*; and for 'the whole of': *She drank all (of) the milk.*

2. Be careful when using *all* and *whole* with negatives. *I couldn't sleep the whole night* means either that I woke up sometimes or that I was awake the whole time. *All these questions cannot be answered* may mean that some of them can be. Prefer *I was awake all night*, and *None of these questions can be answered*, or *Not all these questions can be answered*, whichever you mean.

3. *All* can be used adverbially: *They are all wrong* can mean 'They are completely wrong' or 'All of them are wrong'. Be careful!

almost see nearly

alone/(all) by oneself/on one's own

All of these can mean 'separated from others': *I was (all) alone/(all) by myself/(all) on my own in the house*. Or they can mean 'without help': *I can't carry it alone – it's too heavy*.

aloud see **loud**

also/too/as well

Sentences such as *We also have two children*, or *She's a good skier, too* may mean either 'as well as you, etc.', or 'as well as three dogs and a cat', 'as well as being a brilliant architect'. If the context does not make it clear, they should be phrased differently: *We have three dogs and a cat as well as two children*.

Also is a little more formal than the other words. At the end of a clause, prefer the more common *too* or *as well*. Strictly speaking, any of these words should be placed next to the part of the sentence they refer to. Compare:

The hero has also killed a giant (= as well as rescued the princess).
The hero has killed a giant too (= as well as three dragons).
The hero too has killed a giant (= so the heroine isn't the only one who has killed one).

Too is used in informal short responses: *I volunteer. Me, too!* (= 'So do I', 'I do, too').

Too and *also* (but not *as well*) can come immediately after the subject in rather formal style: *This too shall pass*.

Also can begin a sentence with inverted word order, particularly in newspaper English: *Also present on that memorable occasion were Keats and Shelley*. (See **inversion**.) *(And) also* is sometimes used, rather informally, like *and*: *I want two shirts, (and) also a pair of socks*.

although see **nevertheless.**

American and British English

There are differences in pronunciation, spelling, vocabulary and grammar between these two main varieties of English; but as speakers and writers of one can almost always understand the other perfectly well, it does not matter which you decide to learn and use.

This book is written in the British English of the 1990s. (It is important to say this, because the state of affairs is changing all the time. British English is continually influenced by American English, and to a lesser degree the other way round.) We describe some important differences between British and American usage, where they occur under the various topics discussed.

However, if you are writing in English, you should stick consistently to either

British or American spelling. American spelling is more regular than British spelling, and where there are differences the AmE form is generally shorter. The following list sets out examples of some of the more important differences. For fuller information, consult *Lexicographic Description of English* (Benson, Benson and Ilson: John Benjamins, 1986). The list is set out in three columns: BrE on the left, AmE on the right, and English (common to both) in the middle:

BrE	*English*	*AmE*
-our		**-or**
behaviour		behavior
colour		color
favour		favor
flavour		flavor
honour		honor
humour		humor
vapour		vapor
colourful		colorful
honourable		honorable
favourite		favorite
flavoursome		flavorsome
	coloration	
	humorous	
	humorist	
	honorary	
	vaporize	
	actor	
	author	
colourist		colorist

Notes: These are polysyllabic words mostly of Latin (or French) origin, except for *neighbour/neighbor* and *harbour/harbor*. Both BrE and AmE keep *-or* in 'agent' nouns such as *actor*, *author*, though the spelling *saviour* still competes with *savior* in AmE.

Inflections preserve the distinction. Derivatives of *-our* words keep *-our* except when the suffix is Latin or Greek: *-ary*, *-ation*, *-ize/-ise*, *ist*, and *-ous*. *Colourist/colorist* is an exception.

BrE	*English*	*AmE*
	ae	**e**
	aesthetic	esthetic
	archaeology	archeology
	palaeolithic	paleolithic

Notes: These are mostly of Greek origin. The spellings *encyclopaedia* and *encyclopedia* are found both in BrE and in AmE. AmE seldom uses *e* for *ae* in names, such as *Aeschylus.*

BrE	*English*	*AmE*
oe		**e**
amoeba		ameba
oestrogen		estrogen
homoeopathic		homeopathic

Notes: In such Greek-derived words the likelihood of *oe* in AmE is greater at the beginning of a word: *oestrogen* is more likely than *homoeopathy*. At the beginning of a word, *oe* is pronounced /iː/ but *e* is pronounced /e/. Elsewhere, they are both /iː/. Classical names such as *Oedipus* usually preserve *oe* in AmE. The spellings *foetus* and *fetus* are found in both BrE and AmE. The word is of Latin origin.

BrE	*English*	*AmE*
-re		**-er**
centre		center
litre		liter
fibre		fiber
mitre		miter
sceptre		scepter
meagre		meager
kilometre		kilometer
	theatre	theater
	acre	
	lucre	
	massacre	
	mediocre	
	ogre	
	maker	
	painter	
	writer	
	thermometer	
	sober	
	neuter	
	beleaguer	
	diameter	

Notes: AmE retains *-re* after *c* and *g* (except in *meager*). This prevents confusion (e.g. between *acre* and *acer*) and the mispronunciation of *c* /k/ as *c* /s/, and of *g* /g/ as *g* /dʒ/. Both BrE and AmE have *-er* for agent nouns like *writer*, and for many other words such as *neuter*, *sober*. BrE distinguishes *meter* 'measuring instrument' from *metre* 'unit of measurement'; AmE has *meter* for both.

BrE	*English*	*AmE*
-(n)ce, -(n)se		**-(n)se, -(n)ce**
defence		defense
offence		offense
pretence		pretense

BrE	*English*	*AmE*
	practise (v)	practice (v)
	license (v)	license (v)
	practice (n)	practice (n)
	licence (n)	license (n)

Notes: Whereas BrE uses *-(n)se* for the verbs and *-(n)ce* for the nouns, AmE tends to use *-(n)se* for both, though not invariably. Of course there are other words such as *patience* and *circumstance* for which *-nce* is the only spelling.

BrE	*English*	*AmE*
-lys(e)		**-lyz(e)**
analyse		analyze
paralyse		paralyze
	analysis	
	analyst	
	paralysis	
-ise	**-ize**	

Notes: Some words, such as *advise, capsize*, have only *-ise* or only *-ize*. In most cases, such as *civilise/civilize, organise/organize*, AmE has only *-ize* whereas BrE can choose between *-ize* and *-ise*. The difference extends to all inflections and derivatives (*civilisation/civilization*). Since more words positively require *-ise* than *-ize*, a consistent use of *-ise* will avoid some mistakes. But since *-ize* is common English, its use is more acceptable internationally.

BrE	*English*	*AmE*
	-l	**-ll**
	appal	appall
	distil	distill
	enrol	enroll
	enthral	enthrall
	extol	extoll
	fulfil	fulfill
	instil	instill
	-ll-	**-l-**
	labelled	labeled
	jeweller	jeweler
	counsellor	counselor
	travelling	traveling
	marvellous	marvelous
	quarrelled	quarreled

Notes: Label, jewel etc are all words of more than one syllable ending in a single written vowel followed by *-l*. In BrE, a final *-l* in all such words is always doubled before a derivational or inflectional suffix beginning with a vowel. In AmE, the *-l* is usually doubled only if the last syllable is stressed. So both BrE and AmE make *annulling* (with a vowel ending) but *annulment* (with a consonant ending) from *annul*, which is stressed on the second syllable.

Besides these systematic differences, there are many individual words with BrE–AmE spelling differences. A typical case is the co-occurrence of the common English spelling *plough* with the AmE variant *plow*. But in some cases, BrE makes a distinction where AmE does not. Some examples are:

BrE	*English*	*AmE*
cheque (money)		check
check (elsewhere)		
disk (computers)		disk
disc (elsewhere)		
kerb (roadside)		curb
curb (restrain)		
program (computers)		program
programme (elsewhere)		
tyre (car), tire (v)		tire
	pedlar (itinerant seller), peddler (one who pushes drugs)	peddler

among(st) see **between/among**

an see **a and the (1)**

and see **go (1)**

angry/cross/furious/annoyed/upset

> TYPICAL MISTAKE: **The boss was angry against me.*

In BrE, one is *angry, cross, furious* or *annoyed with* someone or *at* something. Compare:

> *The boss was angry with me.*
> *He was angry at the delay* (AmE has both *angry with* and *angry at* someone).

Angry suggests a strong feeling, and *furious* means 'very angry, violently angry'. *Cross* is a less formal word and not so strong. *Annoyed* means 'fairly angry', but *upset* suggests that you are unhappy, worried or disappointed about something unpleasant.

answers

Here are some useful phrases to be used as short answers:

Good news

'Look, the bar is still open.'

'They've all come home safely.'

'I've passed the exam!'

Oh, good! Thank goodness! Great!

Thank heavens! Thank God!

Congratulations! Well done! Good for yòu!

Bad news

'I'm afraid I can't come to your party.'

That's too bad! What a pity! What a shame. (*Shame* doesn't mean 'disgrace' here.)

'I've run out of stamps.'

How annoying! What a nuisance.

'I've lost my wallet.'

That's terrible. Bad luck! Hard luck!

Rather surprising news

'They got married yesterday!'

You don't say? Really? Good heavens! Good Lord! (My) goodness!/(esp. AmE) Is that rîght?/ sô?/(informal) a fâct? (rise-fall intonation)

'He expects us to pay his hotel bill!'

What a nerve!/(esp. BrE) What cheek!

Thanks

'Thank you very much for helping.'

Not at all. Don't mention it./ (informal) That's OK. (esp. AmE: You're welcome. (informal) No problem.)

Apologies

'I'm sorry.'

It doesn't matter. Never mind. Don't worry. It's/That's all right. (informal: That's OK./ (esp. AmE) No problem.)

Praise

'Well done!'

'What a pretty dress!'

'That was a good speech you made.'

Thank you. Thanks.

Thank you. Oh, thank you.

Thank you. I'm glad you liked it. (And see **thank you**.)

Suggestions and proposals

'Would 4 o'clock suit you?'

'Let's meet at 10.'

'I'd rather go to the circus.'

Yes, that's fine. Yes, 4 o'clock is fine.

All right. Fine! (informal) OK.

Great! What a good idea!

(or) Suit yourself! (can be rude).

Questions; confirmation of facts

'Your phone number is 685–4203, isn't it?'

'The train leaves at 7.30, I think.'

} Yes, that's right.

'Can you swim?' Yes, of course. Of course I can.
'Has he got to stay in bed?' Yes, I'm afraid so. No, definitely/
certainly not.

'Are you cold?' No, I'm fine, thanks.
'Am I right?' Yes, absolutely. Yes, you are. I'm
afraid not.

'Do you agree?' Yes, certainly. Yes, I do.
'Didn't you watch the programme?' Yes (= I did). No (= I didn't).

Requests
'Please hold this rope.' Right/(informal) OK.
'Can you hold this rope for me?' (Yes,) of course. (Yes,) certainly.
'Can I put my coat here?' (Yes,) certainly.

Statements to argue about
'I think the space programme is a waste of money.' (1) You're quite right. I (esp. BrE)
quite/absolutely/entirely agree with
'British TV isn't much good.' you. Absolutely!
(2) You may be right. Perhaps/
Maybe you're right.
(3) I don't entirely agree with you
(there)./(esp. BrE) You're quite
wrong.
(4) (That's) utter nonsense/rubbish!
You're/You must be/ (esp. AmE)
You've got to be joking!

any/some

TYPICAL MISTAKE: *Would you like any beer?*

1. The general rule is that we use *some, somebody, something, somewhere* for positive statements, and *any, anybody, anything, anywhere* for negatives and questions: *I have some work to do. I haven't any work to do.*

But *some*, etc., are often used in questions, if we expect the answer 'yes': *Haven't you some work to do?* (= I'm sure you have). This is particularly true when the questioner is offering something: *Would you like some beer?* (If I say *Do you want any beer?* it sounds as if I am advising you not to have any.) See also **few (2)**; **nonassertive**.

2. There may be a choice between *some, any* and nothing at all. It sometimes does not matter. You can say *I'd prefer wine* (or *some wine*); *I didn't add salt* (or *any salt*). But compare:

You mustn't eat peaches (they give you spots).
You mustn't eat any peaches (we need them all for the party).

apologies

Here are some useful phrases to use when apologizing. For something small, such as bumping into a stranger, you can say: *(I'm) sorry./*(rather formal) *I beg your pardon./*(esp. AmE: *Pardon me/Excuse me.*)

You may want to add some words of explanation: *(I'm) sorry I'm late. I'm very sorry to have been such a nuisance. I'm sorry if I disturbed you.* (It is better not to say that you are *sorry for* something, because that expression usually means that you are sad about someone's unhappiness, as in *I felt very sorry for his poor wife.*)

You may want to apologize for something you are going to do or say: *I'm very sorry to trouble you/Do forgive me for disturbing you, but would you lend me your umbrella?*

Excuse me is a sort of apology, and you use it when attracting the attention of strangers: *Excuse me, isn't this your purse?* You also say *Excuse me* when you want to push past someone in a crowded place. (Americans say it after, as well as before, pushing!) You might also say *Would you excuse me for a moment?* before leaving the room; or *Excuse my not getting up – I've sprained my ankle.* Children at school say *Please may I be excused?* when they want to go to the toilet.

An apologetic answer to a question might be *I'm sorry, but I don't know*, or *I'm afraid not.*

The verb *apologize* and the noun *apology* are used in rather more formal apologies. You apologize *to* someone *for* something: *I wish to apologize for my absence from the meeting.*

If you want someone to apologize to you, you can say *I think you owe me an apology.* (See also **answers.**)

appear see linking verbs

appetite see desire

appointments

You *make* an *appointment*, perhaps to see your dentist. When you have done that, you then *have (got)* an *appointment* (*with* the dentist):

May I make an appointment for a checkup (= an examination) *early next week?* (When you arrive) *I have an appointment at 4.30. My appointment is at/for 4.30. I have a 4.30 appointment.*

appositional clauses see relative clauses

approximately/around see about

arise see happen

as/than

You can say:

> *He's the same age as me. They're richer than us* (rather informal but very common).
> *He's the same age as I. They are richer than we* (formal and rather affected).
> *He's the same age as I am. They're richer than we are* (neutral).

Of course, in the case of *as you, than you,* the word *you* is the same in either case, so there is no problem of formality. Be careful of possible confusion in sentences like *He admires you more than Mary,* which may mean either *than Mary does* or *than he admires Mary.* Say *more than Mary does, more than he does Mary,* according to which you mean.

(For the choice between *as/when/while* something happened, see **when**. For *as/how/like* something, see **[1]like**.)

ask

> TYPICAL MISTAKES: *He asked to me a question. *Let's ask her for the way.*

When you want to know something, you *ask* someone, or you *ask* something. The possible verb patterns are:

> *If he doesn't know, he must ask.*
> *Ask Peter!*
> *He asked about the accident.*
> *'What's this?' she asked.*
> *'Who are you?' she asked him.*
> *He asked (them) where it was.*
> *He asked (me) what to do.*
> *He asked (me) a question* (or, formally, *he asked a question of me*).
> *She asked (me) my name.*
> *I asked (him) the time.*

But when you want something, you *ask for* it, or *ask* someone *for* it: *If he wants help, he must ask (for it).*

If you want to do something, or want someone to do something, the verb patterns are:

> *He asked her to marry him.*
> *He asked her not to bother him.*
> *He asked that the prisoners (should) (not) be released.*
> *I asked (him) if he would carry the baby.*

asking for things

1. When you want something, it is more polite to use the indirect forms *could, might* than the related forms *can, may*; and to add *please*: *Can I/May I/Could I/*(formal) *Might I have some more tea, please?*

I'd like is more polite than *I want*: *I'd like spaghetti, please.*
You might use the direct *Can I* to a friend: *Can I read your letter?*
There are various ways of making a request less 'direct', particularly if you are asking for something that may cause a lot of trouble:

Do you think I could possibly stay the night?
I wonder/I was wondering whether I could possibly stay the night. (Here, the past tense *was wondering* is even more 'indirect' and therefore more polite.)
Is it all right/Do you mind if I open the window?
Have you got/Can you spare a minute? (= I want to speak to you).

2. When you want someone to do something, the rule is the same: do not be too direct. The imperative form of the verb is very direct, so in a hotel you should say *Would you/Could you have this suit cleaned, please?* (Not *Have this suit . . .* Here, *could* is even politer than *would.*) Here are some ways to express wishes more politely:

Can/Could/Would you pass me that glass?
Can/Could/Would you please stop talking?
Would you mind waiting? (This means 'Please wait!' If you said *Do you mind if you have to wait?* it would be a warning that waiting may be necessary.)

For something that may cause a lot of trouble, you could say:

Could you possibly meet the train?
Do you think you could possibly meet the train?
I wonder whether you could possibly. . . .
I was wondering if you could possibly. . . .

A gentle way of making a request is: *I'd rather you didn't smoke in here.*

3. When you want to know something, you may have to ask a stranger. Do not be too direct:

Excuse me! Can/Could you tell me the way to Euston Station?
(formal) *Would you be good enough to tell me the way. . . .*
How do I get to Euston Station, please?
Do you know how to get to. . . .
(esp. BrE) *Am I right for Euston Station?*

You may need to say: *I'm lost! I've lost my way.* The person may answer:

You turn left at the corner and go. . . .
You'll have to go to Bond Street Station and take the Underground to. . . .

You may need to say: *I'm sorry, do you mind repeating that?* Or you might look at your map, and say: *You mean we're HERE and the station is THERE?*

assemblage/assembly

There is seldom any need to use the rare, formal word *assemblage.* You might use it for a group or cluster of things or people; perhaps an *assemblage* of trees or insects. But the process of fitting parts together is usually called *assembly* (uncountable), as with a car *assembly line*. A structure that has been fitted together is an *assembly*, too, as with the power *assembly* in a motor bike. The gathering together of people for a purpose is *assembly* (uncountable), as with the *right of assembly*, and a group of people who have gathered together for legislation, worship, etc., is an *assembly*, as with the *General Assembly* of the United Nations.

at/in/on

1. places

(a) In general, we use *at* for a point and *in* for an area: *at the bus stop; in the bathroom*. In BrE, small towns and villages are more often thought of as a point, and large cities as an area: *He lives at Moreton-in-the-Marsh; he works in London*. AmE tends towards *in* for both. But a small place may be thought of as an area by the people who live there: *Everyone in Moreton likes him*. A large city, or its airport, may be thought of as a point when we speak of global distances: *We refuelled at London on our way to Tokyo*.

(b) Use *in* for general words about someone's residence or workplace, *at* for particular ones: *He lives in a cottage/a caravan/a cave; he lives at 14 Holywell Street*. You can change your money *at a bank*, or shelter from the rain *in a bank* (= inside the building). You can be *at the theatre* (= watching a play) or *in the theatre* (= inside the building, or in the theatrical profession). The British can use *cinema* like that. You use *at* before *church, school, college* to talk about the characteristic activities that go on there: *Billy's at school* (= he's learning or teaching). Americans can also use *in school* in this meaning; and you might hear people complaining about children making a noise *in church*.

(c) Compare the usages set out below.

at	in	on
at (= beside) a table, desk	in an armchair	on a bench, a hard chair
	in a balcony (= upstairs in a theatre)	on a balcony (= outside a house)
knock at/on the door	work in the fields	work on the land
	in the country, countryside	on page 17
	a pain in my stomach	hit him on the head
	(BrE) in the street in Oxford Street	(AmE) on the street on Fifth Avenue
at/on the corner (= where two streets meet)	in the corner (= inside a room)	

2. times

Use *at* for points of time: *at 6 o'clock; at sunset; at bedtime; at* (BrE) (or *during, over*) *the weekend; at Christmas* (= the season, not the day); *at the last moment.* (Note also *at night* (see **night**); *at the time, at such times.*)

Use *on* for days: *on Saturday; on June 8th.* (Note also *on the hour* (= at exactly 3 o'clock, etc.).)

Use *in* for periods of time: *in October; in the afternoon; in* (or *during*) *the last few days.* (For the choice between *on time* and *in time*, see **time (2)**.)

You can use *on* or *at* for stages in a process: *We're still on* (or *at*) *page 17.*

3. at/in/on (times) or nothing at all?

TYPICAL MISTAKE: *She died Christmas day morning.*

Expressions such as *last week, next year, this morning* are used adverbially without *at, in* or *on*: *We'll go there next Monday.* A student might say *We have English second period today*, rather than *in the second period.* Sometimes there is a choice. You can say *They got married the day* (or *on the day*) *war broke out.* Otherwise, use *at, in, on*: *She died on the morning of Christmas day.*

(For the choice between *with/in/on* as in *in pencil, with a pencil, in Swahili*, see **with**. For expressions such as *surprised at, good at*, see **verbal adjectives**; **word and preposition**.)

awake/awaken/wake/waken

Nowadays, *awaken* and *waken* tend to be regular verbs: *(a)waken, (a)wakened*; while *awake* and *wake* tend to be irregular: *(a)wake, (a)woke, (a)woken.* Note that the form *awaked* is now rare. All four verbs can be both transitive and intransitive, and can be both literal and figurative; but the verb *waken* is less common than the other three.

awful/horrible/terrible/frightful

You can use all these words about something bad: *awful/horrible/terrible/frightful accidents.* Older writers tried to confine *awful* to the meaning 'causing awe' (= fear and wonder), but this sense is now literary, and *awesome* is used for it instead. Informally, all these words except *horrible* can mean 'extreme', and the adverbs *awfully, frightfully* can mean 'extremely': *it won't make an awful/a terrible/a frightful lot of difference.*

awhile

This is an adverb: *We're not getting married yet awhile.* *A while* is a noun phrase: *It took quite a while; it took a little while.* Except in the phrase *yet awhile, a while* can almost always replace *awhile.* But in many cases, *awhile* is criticized if it replaces *a while*: *quite a while, a while longer, a while ago.* So when in doubt, use *a while* rather than *awhile.*

back

TYPICAL MISTAKE: *They say nasty things about her at her back.*

At the back of something means 'in the back part of' it, so you can say *We sat at the back of the aircraft*. It also means 'behind' it, so you say *There's a garden at the back of the house*.

But when we speak of a person, then *at their back* means 'supporting' or 'pursuing' them: *He crossed the Alps with an army at his back*.

The right expression for 'without their knowledge' is *behind their back*: *They say nasty things about her behind her back*.

bad(ly) see **adjective or adverb?**

bank

When you *pay* a *cheque* (AmE *check*) *into* your *account*, or *deposit* it *in* your account at a bank, it adds to your *savings*. (You may receive *interest* on your account.) When you want to *draw out/withdraw* money from the bank you *make out* one of the cheques in your *chequebook* (AmE *checkbook*) and the (BrE) *cashier* (AmE *teller*) *cashes* it. From time to time, the bank gives you a computerized *statement* of the cheques paid in and out, and the amount of money remaining. (For the other meaning of *bank*, see **coast**.)

barely see **hardly**

bath

The basin you sit in to wash yourself is a *bath* (AmE *bathtub* or *tub*). When you sit in it you are *bathing*, or *having* (AmE also *taking*) a bath. The apparatus you stand under to wash yourself under running water is a *shower*, and when you use it you are *showering*, or *having/taking* a shower. In BrE the verb *bath* is what you do in a bath: *to bath the baby*; and to *bathe* is to wash a wound or sore place, or else to go swimming. AmE uses *bathe* for both, but Americans don't usually use a verb at all; they give the baby a *bath*, and they go swimming (as the British do too). Note that the word *bathing* comes from both *bath* and *bathe*, and its pronunciation depends on its source verb. (See also **swim**.)

beach see **coast**

bear see **stand**

beat see **win(1)**

become see **linking verbs**

been

1. | TYPICAL MISTAKE: *Have you ever gone to Paris?*

The participle *been* can be used as if it were part of the verb *go*. To have *been* usually means that you have gone there and come back again. Compare:

> *He's been to Paris* (= that's why he was away last week; also, now he knows what Paris is like).
> *He's gone to Paris* (= that's why he's not here now).

2. | TYPICAL MISTAKE: *I don't remember being to that restaurant before.*

You cannot *be to* a place. It is only *been* that is used in that way, so you must say either *remember going to* or *remember having been to*. We use *been to* for a visit, or a series of visits: *I've often been to London*.

before/after

1. If today is Monday, then Wednesday is *the day after tomorrow*, and Saturday was *the day before yesterday*. The expressions *the day after* and *the day before* mean 'the next day' and 'the previous day': *He couldn't go on Monday, so he went the day after* (= Tuesday).

2. If you say *He won't come till/until tomorrow*, it means that he will come tomorrow. If you say *He won't come before tomorrow*, it means not sooner, but perhaps even later.

begin/start/commence

1. The three verbs are used in the same verb patterns. You can *begin/start/commence to do* something (very rare after *commence*), or *doing* it. Avoid using the *-ing* form twice: *He's beginning to cut* (not **cutting*) *the grass.* Avoid the *-ing* form in sentences about the mind or feelings: *She started to realize* (not **realizing*) *the truth.*

2. Prefer *begin* or *start.* *Commence* is very formal, used sometimes in announcements: *The meeting will now commence.* *Start,* but not *begin* or *commence,* is the only one to use before *back, off, out, up: Let's start off with soup;* or for the meaning 'begin a journey or race': *They started (out) for the North;* or about machines: *The car won't start; I'm trying to start the car;* or for 'bring into existence': *to start (up) a music society;* or for 'make a sudden movement': *The loud bang made her start.*

behave see **reflexives(1)**

believe

> TYPICAL MISTAKE: **Do you believe to God?*

You *believe* a fact: *I believe (that) it's raining;* or a person: *'I don't believe you!'* To *believe in* something or somebody is either to think they exist (*I don't believe in Father Christmas*) or to have faith and confidence in them (*She believes in taking lots of exercise*). (See also **think.**)

below/beneath see **under**

bet

This verb is a curiosity; *bet* and the more formal *wager* are the only ones that can take three objects. The following patterns are all correct: *I bet you £5. I bet you we'll win. I'll bet £5 on the next race. I bet we'll win. I bet you £5 we'll win.*

The past and past participle of *bet* are now usually *bet;* the form *betted* is old-fashioned.

better see **sick(3)**

between/among

When you are speaking of only two things or people, or two groups, use *between: I divided the money equally between Lucy and Pauline.*

Use *among* when speaking of more than two, particularly when the number is vague: *The plane disappeared among the clouds. He is among the best of them.* But when we speak of precise relationships or position, *between* is preferred: *Ecuador lies between Colombia, Peru and the Pacific Ocean.*

Use *between* when speaking of action by a group, or of the total effect of several things: *Between them the class managed to raise £200.*

The form *amongst* is esp. BrE, and rather old-fashioned.

big/large/great; high/tall

Big is less formal than *large* and *great*. We seem to prefer *great* for abstract things: *a big* (or *large*) *room/cake/dog/house/city; a great* (informal *big*) *strain/problem/mistake/ success*. A *big* (opposite *little*) or *large* (opposite *small*) thing or person is wide as well as high. It is reasonable to say that a child is *big* (or *tall*) for his or her age, but tall thin people or buildings would not be called *big*. In the same way, a short fat man is not *little*.

In the case of children, *big* (but not *large*) means old, or older. Your *big sister* is older than you are, and your *little brother* is younger: *You'll be able to climb the mountain when you're bigger.* The combinations *great big* and (BrE) *huge great* are possible: *a great big slice; a huge great slice;* but both combinations are informal and rather childish.

High and *tall* are the only words in this list that are used when giving measurements: *a mountain 2000 m. high; a woman only 4 feet tall.* We use *high* (opposite *low*) when thinking of a distance above the ground: *a high shelf; high mountains.* (*High* is not used in this sense about people; a *high official* is high in rank!) We use *tall* (opposite *short*) when thinking of length from top to bottom, particularly when the person or thing is also narrow: *a tall man/tree/tower.* Buildings are called either *tall* or *high*.

billion

This now means 'thousand million' in BrE as well as in AmE. BrE still uses *thousand million*, too. So 3,400,000,000 is nowadays 'three billion, four hundred million' in both BrE and AmE, but sometimes also 'three thousand four hundred million' in BrE. In BrE, *billion* used to mean 'million million', but the word for this larger number is now *trillion* in BrE as well as in AmE. (See also **numbers**.)

bit/little

TYPICAL MISTAKE: **a bit money.*

A *bit* and a *little* are both used with the meaning 'rather', with adjectives and adverbs. A *bit* is rather informal: *The meat's a bit/a little tough.*

These words are not used with plurals: *rather* (not **a bit* or **a little*) *fewer mistakes.* You can use them with verbs: *Wait a bit/a little.* You can use both together: *a little bit less sugar.* In addition, *a bit* and *a little* can mean 'a small amount': *'Milk in your tea?' 'Just a little.'* Before nouns, use either *a little* or *a bit of: a little trouble/money; a bit of trouble/money.*

(For the choice between *little* and *a little, few* and *a few*, see **few**.)

blow see up(2)

boat/ship

Boats are usually smaller than *ships*, but *boat* is often used informally of a large passenger liner, or a cross-Channel steamer. Naval surface vessels above a certain size are *ships*, but a submarine is a *boat*.

border/frontier/boundary

A *border* or (esp. BrE) *frontier* divides two nations; a *boundary* divides, for instance, two farms, or marks the edge of a city. We always speak of the *border* between England and Scotland, or England and Wales, or the USA and Canada or Mexico. In older American history, *the frontier* also meant the edge between settled country and wild country, typically to its west, and in AmE one can speak of crossing the state *line* or going beyond the city *limits*. Note also the phrases *the frontiers of knowledge, the boundaries of good taste*. In BrE, *frontier* is pronounced '*frontier*; in AmE, usually *fron'tier*.

boring see dull

boss see head

both/either/each

Sometimes it does not matter which you use. You can say *Both are* (or *Each/Either is*) *possible*. *Both* is used for two, but not more than two, items: *Both George and I live in Cumbria. We both live in Cumbria.* (Here, *both* implies that we do not live together. *George and I/We live in Cumbria* neither implies nor denies that we live together.)

You can use *both* even if the items are themselves plural: *Both the teacher and the students enjoyed it.* When you speak of two, or more than two, items individually, use *each*. Note the verb forms: *They each enjoy it in a different way. Each of them enjoys it in a different way.*

There are some ambiguities with *both*. A sentence like *Both (of) their daughters are lawyers* might refer to one couple who have two lawyer daughters, or to two people who each have one. Rephrase it as *They each have a daughter who is a lawyer*, or *They have two daughters who are both lawyers*, whichever you mean.

Note the word order and verb forms:

Both (of the) students have done well. They both did well.
Both (the) students have done well. They have both done well.
Each of the students has done well. They each did well.
Each student has done well. They have each done well.

(For sentences like *Each child did his* (or *their*) *best*, see **singular or plural?**)

bother

TYPICAL MISTAKE: *If you need anything, don't bother to ask.*

There is nothing wrong with this sentence grammatically, but its meaning (. . . 'don't ask') is probably just the opposite of what its author intended, which was: *If you need anything, don't hesitate to ask* (THAT sentence means 'Please ask'). The underlying cause of the mistake is probably that *no/not bother* is used typically not in expressions of polite discouragement (*Don't bother to ask*), but in expressions of polite encouragement or reassurance, such as: *It's no bother for me to get you what you need* (= so please ask me). *Don't bother to knock/knocking/about knocking* (just come on in). However, all these expressions remain negative in form. *Don't bother to knock* still means 'Don't knock'.

bow see down

bowl/dish/plate/platter

A *bowl* is deep and round, suitable for holding liquids, flowers, sugar, salad, even goldfish. A *dish* is large, flat, and either round or oval, and food is served from it onto people's plates. It may have a lid. A *plate* is flat, smaller than a dish, and usually round. People eat off it. The word *dishes* can include *bowls, plates, saucers, cups, mugs*, all *crockery* in fact, since after a meal we have to wash, dry, rinse and stack the *dishes* unless, of course, we own a mechanical *dishwasher*. (The expression *wash up* in this sense is BrE only; Americans *do* or *wash the dishes*.) In AmE a large dish or plate, typically oval and flattish, can be called a *platter*. There are *platters* for serving from and *platters* for eating off, as in the phrase *a sea-food platter*.

boy see man

brand see sort

break see tear

bring/fetch/take

TYPICAL MISTAKE: *I'll bring you to Spain with me when I go.*

If you *bring* somebody or something to a place, you have them with you when you come. If you *fetch* somebody or something, you go and get them and bring them back; *bring* and *fetch* end up 'here', with the speaker or hearer. If you *take* somebody or something to a place, you have them with you when you go:

I'll take you to Spain with me when I go.
I'll take/bring him to Spain with me when I go/come to visit you.
She came to my party and brought me a present.
She went to his party and took him a present.
I've forgotten your present – I must run home and fetch it!

British English see American and British English

build/construct

The verb *build* applies typically to things that rise up from the ground and have a roof and walls: *to build a church/a block of flats*. Ships and bridges are also built, and birds build their nests. The verb *construct* can be used formally for all these, too, but it has a wider application where *build* might sound a little odd: *to construct a machine/a maze/a canal/a motorway*. Both *build* and *construct* can be used figuratively. *Build* is apt when speaking of something that needs a foundation: *build a new society/a new identity for oneself*. *Construct* is apt when the emphasis is on fitting parts together: *construct a plot/a theory*.

but see nevertheless

by/with

1. | TYPICAL MISTAKE: **He shot the bird by an arrow.*

Use *by* for the doer of the action in a passive sentence, *with* for the instrument that he used: *He shot the bird with an arrow. The bird was shot with an arrow by a hunter.*

2. | TYPICAL MISTAKE: **She has a daughter from her first husband.*

Both men and women have children *by* (or sometimes *with*) people. But you can say *He has two children from his first marriage.*

café/cafeteria see **restaurant(1)**

call see **name(1)**

can/could

1. | TYPICAL MISTAKE: *Because she worked hard she could pass the exam.*

Can and *could* are used about simple ability: *Can you swim? She could play chess when she was five. I can't cook* (prefer this, rather than *I don't know how to cook*, because cooking is a definite skill. You can use *know how to* for 'finding out' something difficult, as in *She doesn't know how to economize*). In all these situations, *be able to* may be used instead, but *can, could* are shorter and neater. Note also the fixed phrases *as fast as I can; he did what he could.*

    Can and *could* are also used with *see, hear, smell, taste* and *feel*, the verbs of the senses: *I couldn't hear anything.* Also common are: *I can believe/understand that. I can't think/imagine why. Can you guess/remember the answer?* But when we speak of 'achievement through ability', there are some special problems:

(a) *Can* and *could* are used for what actually happens, or happened, only with certain 'quasi-negative' qualifiers that suggest success despite near-failure: *The child can only just reach the table-top* (= it can, but only with difficulty).

(b) *Manage to, succeed in, be able to* are used here too, and elsewhere: *She always manages to pass/succeeds in passing the exams. She was able to pass the exam.* This last sentence is ambiguous, because you can be *able* to do something without actually doing it.

    You can use *can* about the future, but only if the possibility, or impossibility, is known NOW. Compare:

Can you come tomorrow? Are you free?
I hope I'll be able to (not *I can*) *drive a car soon.*

    Expressions like *I hope I can, I think I can* mean 'I hope I have the power, but I don't know yet', rather than 'I hope I will have the power': *I hope I can walk as fast as Jessy* (= we'll soon see!). (For *Can I . . . Could I . . .* see **asking for things.**)

    Note that *can, could* can be used in the passive: *I can't do it; it can't be done.* But *manage to, be able to* and *succeed in* cannot be used in the passive: *I wasn't able to climb the tree. *The tree wasn't able to be climbed. *This dress is able to be washed.*

2. *Can, could* are probably used more than *may, might* about 'permission': *You can* (formal *may*) *go now. He said I could* (formal *might*) *go.* But sometimes it is important to distinguish 'permission' from the other meanings of *can* and *could.* Compare:

> *You can't smoke here* (= there's a rule against it, OR I forbid it).
> *You aren't allowed to smoke here* (= there's a rule).
> *You mustn't smoke here* (= I forbid it, either on my own authority or on behalf of the authorities).

The chief meaning of *may, might* is now 'perhaps'. Compare:

> *I may not go home tomorrow* (= perhaps I won't).
> *I mustn't go home tomorrow* (= I've decided it would be a mistake).
> *I won't be allowed to go home tomorrow* (= it won't be permitted).

3. *Could* is also used like *may, might* to mean 'perhaps': *It could/may/might take a long time.* But *could* suggests power. Compare:

> *Could the Gulf War have been prevented?* (= did anyone have the power?)
> *Might the Gulf War have been prevented?* (= was it possible?)

(For the difference between *may have* and *might have*, see **may/might**.)

Avoid *can, could* where there is any chance of confusion with their other meanings. Compare:

> *The door can be locked* (= it's possible to lock it).
> *The door could be locked* (= it was possible to lock it – *locked* as participle – OR perhaps it is locked – *locked* as adjective).
> *The door may/might be locked* (= perhaps it is locked – *locked* as adjective).

capital letters

The question of whether to use capital letters or not is a complicated one. Here are some general rules:

1. Use capitals for all names. This includes people (*George Washington, Aunt Susan*); human groups and nationalities (*Scandinavians, Buddhists, a French boy*); languages (*Sanskrit*); places (*Asia, Sheffield*); days and months (*Tuesday, February*); holidays and religious festivals (*Easter*); trade names (*Honda, Kleenex*); and institutions (*the British Museum, Radio Three, Cambridge University*).

2. Titles usually have capitals for the first word and all other main words: *New Statesman & Society* (magazine); *Aspects of the Theory of Syntax* (book); *The English-Speaking World* (book) (but: *His name is known throughout the English-speaking world*).

3. Use capitals for *God*, the *Lord*, the *Almighty*. It is not wrong, but rather old-fashioned, to use capitals for pronouns (*Thou, He*) referring to him.

4. Human titles are usually capitalized even when incomplete: *the Queen; His Holiness; the Manager regrets . . .; The Royal Society has announced. . . .*

5. The same word may, of course, be used both in a general sense and as a name. Compare:

He went to college.	*He went to Trinity College, Dublin.*
That building is a school.	*It is Newcastle High School.*
after the war	*after the Second World War*
an old church	*the Church of England*
to turn left	*the political Left*
to drive east	*the Far East*
a narrow street	*Oxford Street*
a democratic party	*the Democratic Party*

6. The following are not capitalized: seasons (*spring*) and verbs derived from nouns (*pasteurized milk*). In the names of things called after people or places, possessives keep their capitals (*Bright's disease*). Other such multi-word names may include capitals (*Venetian red*) or not (*venetian blinds*). Single-word names of such things tend not to be capitalized (*cardigan, dahlia, wellingtons*), but sometimes are (*Wellingtons*). Consult a dictionary.

captive see prisoner

capture see conquer

car

To start a car, you have to switch on the *ignition*, and may have to pull out the *choke* before using the *starter*; all these are on the *dashboard*. Of course, you must make sure there is *petrol* (AmE *gas* or *gasoline*) in the *tank*, unless the car runs on *diesel* oil. You drive it by *steering* it with the *steering wheel*, with one foot for the *clutch* and the other for the *brake* or the *accelerator*. You *change gear* (AmE also *shift gears*) by moving the *gear lever* (AmE *gear shift*). You see where you are going through the *windscreen* (AmE *windshield*), and by looking in the *rear-view mirror* and the *wing mirror* (AmE *side(-view) mirror*). The *speedometer* tells you how fast you are going, and the *mileometer* (AmE *odometer*) tells you how far you have gone. Before turning left or right you use the direction *indicators* (AmE *directional signals* or *turn signals*). If it rains you use the *windscreen wipers* (AmE *windshield wipers*). When it gets dark you turn on the *sidelights* (AmE also *parking lights*) and the *headlights*. You can *dip* (AmE *dim*) the headlights if another car approaches. You carry luggage, etc., in the *boot* (AmE *trunk*). In Britain, most states of the USA and many other countries you are now obliged by law to wear a *seat belt*.

You can keep your car in your *garage* (pronounced '*garage* in BrE and *ga'rage* in AmE) or park it in a ground-level *car park* (AmE *parking lot*) or multi-storey *car park* (AmE *garage*), probably in one of many marked-out *parking spaces*. (At a country picnicking place you may see the sign *Parking Area*.)

There are many ways in which a car can *break down*. It may get a *puncture* (AmE also *blow-out*), a *flat tyre* (AmE *flat tire* or *flat*); or the electric *battery* may go flat. To look at the engine, you open the *bonnet* (AmE *hood*).

carry

1. carry/wear

When you *carry* something, you may hold it in your arms or on your back: *to carry a suitcase/a child.* But you may also have it with you on your body, or in a pocket or handbag, wherever you go: *to carry a gun/a lot of cash/an organ-donor card.* You can *carry* clothing, jewellery and watches *with* you, in your suitcase or handbag for example, but you *wear* the clothes, jewellery and watches you have *on: She wore a hat on her head* (but *an earring in her ear*).

2. carry out/carry on

To *carry out* something is to 'perform' it until it is finished, to 'complete' it: *to carry out a survey.* To *carry out* a duty or promise is, similarly, to 'fulfil' it: *to carry out instructions/a threat.* To *carry on* something is to 'perform' or 'continue' it, but with no suggestion of 'finishing' it: *to carry on a war/a correspondence/a tradition.*

cause see chance

centre/middle

> TYPICAL MISTAKE: *He drove down the centre of the road.*

It often does not matter whether you use *centre* (AmE *center*) or *middle* in their literal sense: *a bowl of roses in the centre/middle of the table.* But *centre* is particularly used for an exact point, *middle* for something vaguer: *the centre of the circle; the middle of the forest* (though we speak of the *city centre*). *Centre* is not usually used of long narrow things, such as roads.

certain(ly) see sure

chance/opportunity/possibility; occasion/cause/reason

1. > TYPICAL MISTAKE: *I was so busy I had no occasion to talk to her.*

Both *chance* and *opportunity* can mean a favourable time when something becomes possible. If you *have the chance* or *the opportunity of doing* something, or *to do* it, it becomes luckily possible for you: *I had the chance/opportunity of visiting Paris. I was so busy I had no chance/opportunity to talk to her. Chance*, but not *opportunity*, can mean *possibility*. You do not *have a possibility*, it just exists: *There's a chance/*(more formal) *a possibility that I'll see her.*

An *occasion* can be a time when something happens: *We met on several occasions.* An *occasion* is also a person's *reason* for doing something: *I had occasion/reason to visit Paris.*

The *reason for* an event is the explanation of why it happened; and people have *reasons for* what they do. The *cause of* an event is the thing that produces it or makes it happen. Sometimes you can use either word: *Technical failure was the cause of/the reason for the explosion.* Sometimes you can use only *reason: She gave no reason for leaving.*

2. The expression *by chance* means 'by accident': *I met him quite by chance in the supermarket.*

character *see* **countable and uncountable nouns**

charge for/with/that

> TYPICAL MISTAKES: *They charged him for murder. *They charged £5 from me.

You *charge* somebody money *for* something they have bought, or received, from you: *He charged me £200 for painting the room. They charge £2 admission.* To accuse somebody of a crime is to *charge* them *with* it: *They charged him with murder. Charge that* can mean 'allege that' something bad is true: *The actress charged that the newspaper had lied* (= she accused it of lying).

chief *see* **head**

chips/crisps

Long strips of potato fried in deep fat and eaten hot are called *chips* in BrE and *French fries* or *French fried potatoes* in AmE (and sometimes in restaurants in Britain). Very thin discs of fried potato, sold in packets to be eaten cold, are *crisps* or *potato crisps* in BrE and *chips* or (more usually) *potato chips* in AmE.

citizen/subject

There is today no difference between the legal rights and responsibilities of a *citizen* and those of a *subject*. Republics have *citizens*. A monarchy, such as Britain, may use the word *subject* as well as the word *citizen*, but *citizen* is what appears on the modern British passport.

city/town

In Britain, the sovereign grants a *town* the right to call itself a *city*, while in the USA the same right is conferred by each state. In smaller places, whether they are technically cities or not, we tend to speak of the *town centre*, while larger places such as Birmingham are said to have a *city centre*. The chief administrative building is the *town hall* or (particularly in the USA) *city hall*. London has one town hall for each urban borough.

clean see **tidy**

client see **patient**

climb see **down**

cloth

Two rather more formal words for cloth are *fabric* and *material*; *textile* is more technical, and *stuff* is old-fashioned. But remember that both *material* and *stuff* may also mean substances in general: *'What's that brown stuff in the saucepan?' 'It's gravy.'*

clothes

1. | TYPICAL MISTAKE: *I have three clothes that need washing.* |

Clothes is a plural noun, and it cannot be used with numbers. You must say *three garments*, or *three items of clothing* (both rather formal), or more likely *two shirts and a skirt*.

2. | TYPICAL MISTAKE: *She put on her oldest cloth.* |

Cloth is what *clothes* are made of, and *clothes* are what you wear. A *cloth* (plural *cloths*) is a piece of cloth, or a kind of cloth: *I washed the car with a cloth.*

coast/shore/seashore/bank/shoreline/seaside/beach/coastline

These are all words for the place where land and water meet. *Shore* is the usual word for the edge of the sea, and the only one when speaking of a lake: *walking along the shore* (or the *seashore* or *shoreline*); *the eastern shore of Lake Michigan*. But rivers, streams, canals, etc. usually have *banks*, though one can also speak of the *riverside*, or use *canal-side* as an adjective: *a canal-side picnic; the banks of the Mississippi; Riverside Drive* (by the Hudson River in Manhattan). If you are *in* a river, swimming or rowing for example, you may speak of its *banks* or (if it is very wide) *shores*. If you are *by* a river you are on the river *bank*.

Small ponds and pools, including swimming-pools, have *sides*: *a pool-side party*.

The *seaside* is the edge of the sea regarded as a holiday place. AmE can also use *seashore* like that, but far more readily as a noun than as an adjective: *a week at the seaside* (AmE also *seashore*); *seaside resorts* (both BrE and AmE). A *beach* is a sandy or stony area of smooth shore: *sunbathing on Mediterranean beaches*. In Ireland, it is often called the *strand*.

The *coast* of a country is the part near the sea; or its edge as seen from a distance, or from the point of view of weather or of naval defence: *villages on the coast*. In the USA, the *East Coast* (or *Eastern Seaboard*, esp. south of New England) is the Atlantic coast; the *West Coast* is the Pacific coast, particularly California. *The Coast* is the West Coast, so someone who moves from Chicago to the Coast moves west, not east. Americans speak of *coast-to-coast* travel, or broadcasts.

The *coastline* is the shape of the coast on a map, or as seen from the sea or air: *a rugged coastline*.

coffee shop see restaurant(1)

colour

In questions about the *colour* (AmE *color*) of something, you ask *What colour is it?* (not **has it?*) The answer is usually *It's red* (etc.) rather than *red in colour* or *a red colour*.

come see go(1); linking verbs

commas

The use of the comma is a complicated subject, which we will not discuss in full. Here are three of the more common problems:

1. separating commas

> TYPICAL MISTAKE: **The weather, however made it impossible.*

Commas can separate a part of the sentence from the rest: *And now, ladies and gentlemen, let me introduce our speaker. As a consequence, he had to apply for a new passport.* (An important use of the separating comma is to distinguish between restrictive and non-restrictive constructions. See **relative clauses**.) If the part to be separated from the rest comes in the middle of the sentence, there must be either two commas or none. To leave out one is like leaving out one of a pair of brackets. Do not use one comma between a subject and its verb, or between a verb and its object. Use two or none: *Nobody knew what he wanted. *Nobody knew, what he wanted. Nobody knew, until later, what he wanted. The weather, however, made it impossible.*

2. commas in numbers

Commas are often omitted in four-figure numbers. Write *1000* or *1,000*. Otherwise, use a comma between groups of three numbers (*8,987,401*) except in dates (*the year 1807*), in page numbers (*page 1771*), and in scientific and mathematical work, where spaces are used instead (*3 400 500*).

3. unacceptable combinations

In English the following combinations are unacceptable nowadays, and should be changed as shown:

(a) *, (. . .), as in . . . *praised Walt Whitman, (1819–92), an American poet,* which should become (. . .), as in . . . *praised Walt Whitman (1819–92), an American poet.*
(b) *–. . .–,* as in . . . *praised Walt Whitman – the author of Leaves of Grass –, an American poet,* which should also become (. . .), as in . . . *praised Walt Whitman (the author of Leaves of Grass), an American poet.*

There are other possible solutions, but they are all either controversial or complicated.

4. For the use of commas in letters, see **letters**.

commence see begin

commit

> TYPICAL MISTAKE: *They made a burglary.*

To do something wrong is to *commit* it: *to commit a sin/a crime/a burglary/a motoring offence.* You *make* a mistake or an error, but you *commit* or *make* a blunder.

common/frequent/usual

Things that exist in large numbers are *common*: *Miller is a common name.* Events that happen often are *frequent*: *She was a frequent visitor* (= she came often). Things or events that are ordinary, that recur regularly, or that happen more often than not are *usual*: *I got up at the usual time.*

comparatives

1. more or -er?

One-syllable adjectives and adverbs form their regular comparatives and superlatives with *-er, -est*: *hot, hotter, hottest.* Those with three or more syllables use *more* and *most*: *ridiculous, more ridiculous, most ridiculous.* For those with two syllables, there is a choice: *polite, politer, politest* (or *more/most polite*). The exceptions are:

(a) participles never use *-er, -est* however short they are: *tired, more tired, most tired; tiring, more tiring, most tiring*.
(b) hyphenated adjectives compounded with participles (*kind-hearted, hard-working*) can often take *-er, -est* as well as *more, most*: *kinder-/kindest-hearted* or *more/most kind-hearted*.
(c) three-syllable adjectives beginning with *un-* can use *-er, -est*: *untidy, untidier, untidiest* or *more/most untidy*.
(d) *-er* is never used for comparing two adjectives with each other: *She was more sad* (not **sadder*) *than angry* (or *She was sad more/rather than angry*). (See also **more**.)

2. For mistakes such as **elder than, *more superior*, see **elder.**

compass points

> TYPICAL MISTAKE: **Milan is in the north of Naples.*

Milan and Naples are two separate places. Compare:
> *Milan is north* (or *to the north*) *of Naples.*
> *Milan is in the north of Italy.*

complaining

A typical complaint is *Waiter, there's a fly in my soup!* If someone seems to be in trouble, you might say: *What's wrong? What's the matter/the trouble/the problem?*
The person might reply: *There's something wrong with/something the matter with this pipe. The trouble/The problem is that this pipe is frozen.*

comprise/consist of (or in)/be composed of/constitute/ include/contain

> TYPICAL MISTAKES: **The play comprises of five acts. *Water is comprised of oxygen and hydrogen.*

Although many English speakers say and even write such things, they are considered incorrect. Correctly, when a whole thing is completely made up of several parts, it *comprises, consists of*, or *is composed of* them: *A chess set comprises/ consists of/is composed of 32 chessmen. The play comprises five acts. Water consists of/is composed of hydrogen and oxygen.*

When there is only one ingredient, *comprise* is not used: *Ice consists of/is composed of frozen water.* (Do not use *comprise* in the passive, as in **A chess set is comprised of 32 chessmen*, or *32 chessmen are comprised *by/??in a chess set.*) When several parts add up to a whole, they *compose* or *constitute* it: *32 chessmen compose/constitute a chess set* (do not use *comprise* here).

When a whole is only partly made up of one or more parts, it *includes* or *contains* it or them: *A chess set includes/contains four knights. Water contains hydrogen.* (Do not use *include* for the whole list, as in **includes 32 chessmen*. That is the proper place for *comprise*; but *contain* is sometimes used like that, as in *Water contains hydrogen and oxygen.*) Passive sentences with *contained* and *included* often use *in* rather than *by*: *Four knights are included/contained in a chess set.*

The rare but elegant *consist in* is used typically with abstract ideas or *-ing* forms: *Courage consists in showing grace under pressure.*

concern see **countable and uncountable nouns**

conclusion see **end**

conditionals

1. | TYPICAL MISTAKE: **If it will rain, we'll stay indoors.*

We are traditionally taught not to use a future tense in the *if*-clause of a conditional sentence, and this is usually good advice. The correct forms are: *If it rains, we always stay indoors. If it rains, we'll stay indoors.*

But the situation is really more complicated. The following are perfectly good English: *If it's going to rain* (= if that's true now) *we won't go out. If the lava will reach the town, we must evacuate the inhabitants now. If you WILL play* (= if you insist on playing) *your radio so loud, I'm going out.*

2. | TYPICAL PROBLEM: *?If he was a fly, he could walk on the ceiling.*

Although many English speakers do say this, we are traditionally taught to use *if he were* (etc.) in the *if*-clause of an 'unreal' condition. The correct forms are: *If he were a fly, he could . . . ; If I were you, I would/should . . . ; If it rained/should rain/were to rain, we'd. . . .* (For the form *Were it to rain*, see **inversion**.)

3. | TYPICAL MISTAKES: **If it would rain, we'd stay indoors. *If it would have rained, we'd have stayed indoors.*

Although many English speakers use *'d* in such constructions (*?if he'd have come . . .*) we are taught not to use *would* in the *if*-clause, and again this is usually good advice. The usual correct forms are: *If it rained, we'd stay . . . ; If it had rained, we'd have stayed. . . .* But the following is also perfectly correct: *If it had rained, the road would be wet now.*

4. | TYPICAL PROBLEM: *?I would appreciate it/be grateful if you leave now.*

The *would* here can be interpreted as simply a politer equivalent of *will* or *shall*, and therefore as introducing 'politeness' rather than 'unreality'. This interpretation justifies the use of *leave* rather than *left* in the *if*-clause. However, it would be quite correct to transform this sentence into a typical 'unreal' conditional: *I would appreciate it/be grateful if you left now.*

conquer/invade/overrun/capture

TYPICAL MISTAKE: **The Normans captured England in 1066.*

An enemy first *invades* a country, and may then *overrun* it and successfully *conquer* it, as the Normans did England. Individual towns and people are *captured*.

construct see build

consist (of, in)/constitute/contain see comprise

content/contented see pleased

control see false friends

convince

TYPICAL MISTAKE: **I tried to convince him where he was wrong.*

The correct patterns are:
> *I tried to convince him that he was wrong.*
> *I tried to convince him of his mistake.*

You will also hear *convince* used with an infinitive verb, to mean 'persuade somebody to do something': *I tried to convince him to buy a new car.* This is not thought to be quite such good English, but is criticized less in the USA than in Britain.

cooking

A modern gas or electric *stove,* or (esp. BrE) *cooker,* has gas *burners* or electric *hotplates* or *rings* on top. That is where you *boil* food such as potatoes, in water which you afterwards throw away; or *stew* food such as apples, when you eat the whole contents of the pot; or *fry* food such as fish, in hot fat or oil. *Simmering* is very slow boiling. *Steaming* is cooking food inside a container, so that the water does not touch it. *Braising* is cooking meat slowly in a pot with a little fat and water.

The stove also has a *grill* (AmE *broiler*) where steaks are *grilled* (AmE also *broiled*) under direct heat, and bread is *toasted.* The part of the stove called the *oven* is for *baking* bread and cakes, or *roasting* a large piece of meat. *Fried* potatoes are done on top of the stove, but *roast* potatoes are cooked in the oven with their skins off, usually in the fat of a piece of meat that is also being roasted. Both *roast* and *roasted* are used as adjectives, but *roasted* seems to be used mostly for things roasted over an open fire rather than in an oven: *roast beef; roast(ed) chestnuts. Baked* potatoes or *baked* apples are cooked in the oven with their skins on. *Sauté(d)* potatoes are fried after being boiled. (See also **chips.**)

correct see repair

cost

1. cost/price

> TYPICAL MISTAKE: *What's the cost of this jacket?*

The *price* of a thing is what you have to pay for it; what it *costs: He asked the price of the jacket. He asked what it cost.* When we pay for a service rather than a thing, we speak of the *cost: the cost of a holiday.* (See also **pay.**)

2. You buy and sell things *for* a particular amount of money: *You can get a jacket for £10 in the sale.* But when we mention also the amount of something that is sold, we can use *at* as well as *for: They sell nuts at/for 50p a pound.*

countable (or count) **and uncountable nouns**

1. The following fairly common nouns are always uncountable, except perhaps in some very rare, technical, or old-fashioned senses.

> TYPICAL MISTAKE: *He gave me a good advice/good advices.*

advice	furniture	money
ammunition	garbage	news
artillery	harm	permission
attention	hearsay	progress

baggage	information	rubbish
behaviour (AmE behavior)	jewellery (AmE jewelry)	scenery
blame	know-how	slang
bread	laughter	stationery
cash	legislation	thunder
cutlery	lightning	underwear
equipment	luggage	weather (except
fun	machinery	for the phrase
	mail	*in all weathers*)

2. The following fairly common nouns are always countable. A typical mistake is *She never makes mistake* (this should be *a mistake* or *mistakes*).

accident (except in *by accident*)
bath
contract
lie
mistake (except in *by mistake*)
name (except in *by name, in name*)
price (except in *in price*, or in such contrasts as *Price is more important than quality*)

3. Some nouns that are usually uncountable have a common countable sense. This is true of the names of meals. Compare:

What time is lunch?
They're serving a cold lunch after the meeting.

4. Finally, here is a list of common nouns that may cause particular difficulty:

accommodation Uncountable in BrE, but AmE can use the plural: *to rent office accommodation in London*; (AmE) *tourist accommodations on the boat.*

-ache Nouns ending with *-ache* are uncountable when we speak of the general condition, but can be countable (particularly in AmE) when they mean a single attack of pain: *sufferers from backache/toothache; I've got a stomachache/(esp. AmE) a toothache.* The exception is *headache*, always countable: *He gets terrible headaches.*

character Uncountable when it means 'personality, nature', countable when it is somebody in a book, play, or film: *The two brothers are very different in character. Becky Sharp is a character in 'Vanity Fair'.*

concern Uncountable when it means 'anxiety', countable when it means a business company: *There's no cause for concern. These little restaurants are mostly family concerns.*

credit Uncountable when it means 'deserved praise', or a period of time before you need to pay for goods you have bought. Countable when it means a unit of university study, and countable (singular only) when it means a cause of honour: *We can't claim much credit for her success. You need six more credits to get your degree. He's a great credit to the school.*

damage Uncountable when it means 'harm', plural in the sense of money that one must pay for causing harm: *The storm caused considerable damage to the crops. The court awarded the victim £5000 in damages.*

dress Uncountable when it means 'clothes', countable when it is a woman's one-piece outer garment: *My brother prefers to wear national dress. She put on a clean cotton dress.*

fever Uncountable when it means the general condition, countable (singular only) when it means a high body temperature: *The disease is characterized by fever and vomiting. She has a very high fever.*

fruit Usually uncountable, unless we are speaking in the strict botanical sense, or of different kinds of fruit: *to earn money picking fruit; The potato is not a fruit; jam made of three different summer fruits.*

fuss Uncountable for the general condition, countable (singular only) for an instance of it: *He stamped my papers without much fuss. He made rather a fuss about doing it.*

grass Uncountable except in the botanical sense: *Keep off the grass; a bunch of dried grass(es).*

hair The mass of stuff that grows on your head is uncountable, but one 'thread' of it is countable: *The baby hasn't got much hair yet. Waiter! There's a hair in my soup.*

help Uncountable when it means 'assistance', often countable (singular only) when it means somebody or something that helps: *She needs help to go to the bathroom. I find this insecticide a great help/a lot of help.*

knowledge Usually uncountable, but we speak of somebody's having 'a knowledge of' something that they know: *advances in medical knowledge; He has a good knowledge of tax law.*

nonsense Usually uncountable, but in BrE *a nonsense* is something muddled or silly: *computers printing out nonsense;* (BrE) *The large turn-out made a nonsense of the seating arrangements.*

pain Uncountable in the sense of the general condition, countable when we speak of a particular sensation: *He was in considerable pain. She complains of pains in her legs.* (See also **pain.**)

paper Uncountable unless it means a newspaper, an examination paper (BrE), or an essay. *Papers* are documents: *a piece of paper;* (BrE) *a difficult history paper; 'May I see your papers?' said the officer.*

pleasure Uncountable when it means a feeling of satisfaction, countable when it means something that you enjoy: *She gets a lot of pleasure out of her job. Doing the crossword is one of his few pleasures.*

rest Uncountable for the general condition, countable (usually singular) for a period of resting: *She needs rest after her illness. I had a short rest after lunch.*

seed Uncountable in large quantities, countable when there are only a few: *a sack of grass seed; to grow a few seeds in a saucer.*

shock Uncountable for the medical condition, countable for something that upsets you: *He's in hospital suffering from shock. Her death was a great shock to us all.*

surprise Countable when it means an unexpected event, uncountable for the feeling that the event causes: *His arrival was a lovely surprise. I heard of his resignation without much surprise.*

temperature Countable or uncountable when it means heat in general, countable (singular only) when it means a high body temperature: *The greenhouse effect is a rise in atmospheric temperature. If you've got a temperature you'd better stay in bed.*

toast Uncountable for toasted bread, countable for a ceremonial drink: *baked beans on (a piece/slice of) toast; We drank/proposed a toast to the Queen.*

treatment Uncountable when it means medical attention, countable for a method or drug used: *They get free dental treatment; a new treatment for asthma.*

work Uncountable when it means 'employment', countable when it is something produced, particularly in the arts: *looking for work; the works of Shakespeare* (see also **work**).

course see **undergo**

craving see **desire**

crisps see **chips**

critic

A *critic* may be someone who *criticizes* things, is *critical* of them, and writes or speaks *critically* of them. The *criticism* of such a critic is all about what is bad or wrong. But *criticism* can also refer to more general evaluation that is as much about what is good or correct as about what is bad or wrong: *literary/art/music criticism.* People whose profession is that kind of criticism are also called critics: *an art/a music/a film/a literary/a theatre critic.* Such critics *review* art, music, writing, etc. In their *reviews* they may be critical of, or criticize, what they review, but they may also praise it: *The book got bad/good reviews; it got a good press.* Something that gets good reviews is *a success with the critics,* or *a critical success.*

A *critique* of/about a subject may praise the subject, but is more likely to criticize it: *He published a critique of Marxism.*

criticism

Here are some things to say if you want to criticize someone in a friendly way, without being rude:

> *That doesn't look quite right. Why don't you . . . ?*
> *If I were you I'd. . . .*
> *It might be better to. . . .*
> *May I make a suggestion? Why not . . . ?/How about . . . ?/What about . . . ?/Suppose you. . . .*
> *I like the colour, but I'm not sure about. . . .*
> *I don't think you should have. . . .*
> *Perhaps you were wrong to. . . .*
> *It's a pity you didn't. . . .*

cross see **angry**

cruise see **journey**

cry see **weep**

cushion see **pillow**

customer see **patient**

cut see **drop**

damage see **countable and uncountable nouns**

dark/darkness

The dark is any place where there is no light (literally or figuratively): *sitting in the dark; I'm still in the dark about her intentions.* We also say *after dark, before dark,* meaning the time when night begins: *to get home before dark; to go out after dark. Darkness* is absence of light: *The room was in total darkness.*

dates

1. days and months

When we speak of a date, we say: *the third of May,* or *May the third* (less common), or (AmE) *May third. 'When are you leaving?' 'On the third'* (not *the three*).

When we write it, we always use figures, not words: *3 May 1993,* or *3rd May 1993* (BrE, more old-fashioned), or *May 3(rd), 1993,* or *3/5/1993.* But this last may be confusing, since the Americans put the months first, so that the British will read it as *3 May* and the Americans as *March 5!*

2. years

Written: *1993, 1066, 1789* (no commas).

Spoken: *nineteen ninety-three, ten sixty-six, seventeen eighty-nine.* (See also **numbers(5)**.)

day see **night**

decrease see **drop**

defeat see **win(1)**

departure

When you are going away, you can say: *Well, I'm afraid I must be off now. I'm afraid I must be going/I've got to go. See you!* (See **goodbye**.)

desire/appetite/craving/lust

> TYPICAL MISTAKE: *a desire of succeeding.*

One feels or has a desire *for* something, or *to do* or *to be* something: *a strong desire for success/to succeed.* One can also have a desire *that* something should happen: *a desire that everything should be the way it had been.*

Appetite is desire *for* physical things, particularly food: *The hard work gave us an appetite for dinner.* One can *work up a hearty appetite*, or *have a healthy appetite.*

A *craving* is usually a strong desire *for*, or *to do* or *to be*, something that one would be better without: *a strong craving for cigarettes/to be admired.*

Lust is a very strong word, showing disapproval, and used particularly about sexual desire: *He gazed at her with shameless lust; the unbridled lust for power.*

dessert see pudding

different

1. different from/to/than

It is always correct to say that something is *different from* something else. You will also hear some British speakers say *different to*, and some Americans say *different than*, but these are not considered to be quite such good English: *My job is quite different from/?to/?than his.*

?Different than can be followed by a clause: *Things are different than they used to be.* According to the traditional rule, this would have to become: *Things are different from what/how they used to be.* But you can, of course, say *These two plants are more different (from each other) than I thought.* Note that *similar to* and *dissimilar to* are correct. These rules apply also to derived adverbs: *He behaves differently from me. He behaves similarly to me.* According to the traditional rule, *He behaves differently here than he did there* would have to become *He behaves differently here from how he did there*, or simply *He behaves differently here from there.*

2. different/(an)other/various

(a) You cannot use *different* to mean 'additional'. Use *(an)other*, but notice that it can also mean 'not the same'. *Let's have another drink. Where's the other girl?*

(b) Use *different* to mean 'not the same', but in the plural make it clear whether the things are different from each other or from something else. *His two sons are very different* has two meanings. To make it clear that things are different from each other, you may prefer another word: *They're a different couple* (= from the people we saw yesterday). *They're an ill-matched/a disparate couple* (= unlike each other).

(c) Do not use *different* to mean 'more than one'. You will hear things like *?Different people have noticed it*, but it is confusing and not very good English. Use *various/ several/separate: Several people have noticed it.*

difficult/hard

Often you can use either word: a *difficult* (or *hard*) *language/exam/choice*. But a *difficult life* is one with many problems, while a *hard life* is also tiring and unpleasant, and *hard times* implies poverty. *Difficult work* needs skill, *hard work* is strenuous, and a *hard worker* works hard. A *difficult person* is tiresome, but a *hard person* is cold and unsympathetic.

diminish see drop

director see head

discover see invent

dish see bowl

distant see far(2)

distinguished see famous

disturb/intrude

If you are interrupting someone, you can say *Am I disturbing you?* or *Am I intruding?* But *disturb* is a transitive verb, so you cannot say **Am I disturbing?* (though a sign outside a hotel bedroom can read *Do not disturb*). The adjective *disturbing* is used in contexts like *This news is very disturbing.*

do

1. do/make

English has two verbs here, where many languages have only one. In general, one *does* actions, but *makes* things that did not exist before. Compare:

> *to do the shopping/my exercises/some repairs* (= actions)
> *to make a cake/a fire/a model aircraft* (= things)

Do is often a general word for some appropriate action: *to do* (= brush, comb) *my hair*; *to do* (= clean, brush) *your teeth*; *to do* (= prepare, cook) *food/drinks*:

> *'I'll do* (BrE = attend to) *you now,' said the hairdresser.*
> *'I'll do* (BrE slang = hurt, punish) *you,' said the gunman.*

Note the useful phrase *What's . . . doing? What's this button doing in my coffee?* (= why is it there?). The two verbs are used in many expressions about which there is no rule:

do

one's best
business
the cleaning
a course of study
damage
a dance
(BrE) a deal
a degree (= in physics, etc.)
the dishes (= BrE 'wash up')

one's duty
evil
a favour
the gardening
good (= good deeds)
a good turn
harm
one's homework
the housework
the ironing
a job

justice to somebody/ something
somebody proud
a puzzle
research
the washing
(BrE) the washing-up
work
one's worst
wrong

make

an accusation
arrangements
an attempt
a bed (= arrange the bedclothes)
the best of something
a change
a choice
a comment
(AmE) a deal
a decision
a demand
a difference
a discovery
an effort
an estimate
an exception
an excuse
a face
a fool of somebody
a fortune
friends with somebody

fun of somebody
a fuss
a gain
a gesture
good (= become successful)
a guess (also *have a guess*)
a habit of doing something
haste
an impression on somebody
a good job of something
laws
a living
a loss
a meal
love
a mess
a mistake
money
a movement

a noise
nonsense of something
an offer
peace
a phone call
a plan
a profit
progress
a promise
a purchase
a recommendation
a remark
a request
room for somebody/ something
sense
a statement
a speech
a suggestion
trouble
use of something
war

(For the choice between *make* and *take*, see **take**. For *one's own doing/making*, see **own(2)**. See also **commit**; **make**.)

2. You will very often hear some British speakers saying things like this: *I said I'd pay, and I will do. I don't know whether I'll come, but I might do.* It is considered better English to leave out *do, done, doing* here, and to say simply *I will, he could have*, etc.

down

Some verbs can be combined with *down* without changing their meaning:

The apples are dropping (down) from the tree.
Mind you don't fall (down)!

It is not wrong, but unnecessary, to use *down* in those sentences, since the verbs *drop* and *fall* both imply 'down'. *Down* is never used in the figurative meanings of these verbs: *Prices fell/dropped* (not **down* here).

But with some verbs, to add *down* is to change the meaning: To *bow to* something is simply to 'accept' it. To *bow down* is to show enormous respect: *I bow to your greater experience. I refuse to bow down to our enemies.*

To *climb* something is to go up it. You must add *down* if that is what you want to say: *to climb a tree/a ladder; to climb down the cliff.*

To *come* or *go down* to somewhere means to travel south, or (BrE) away from London, another principal city, or a university (specifically Oxford or Cambridge). (Compare **up**.) Otherwise, use *come* or *go* alone: *When did you come to Britain?* (not *down* here, unless you came from Iceland!).

To *settle* somewhere is to go and live there: *The family settled in Vancouver.* To *settle down* is to establish a quiet home, or to become used to a way of life: *to get married and settle down; She soon settled down in her new school.*

To kill or wound people, or creatures, with a gun is to *shoot* them. The combination *shoot down* is usually used of flying aircraft, not birds. If you *shoot down* a person it suggests that they were running away, and fell down when shot. If you *shoot down* an idea (an informal figurative use), you refute it. (See also **up**.)

dress see countable and uncountable nouns

drinking

When offering someone an alcoholic drink in your home, you might say: *Would you like/Do you fancy/Can I get you/Shall we have a drink?* At a pub, you say *What'll you have?* (After all, at a pub you are expected to drink SOMETHING. People who go to pubs together generally take turns buying a *round* of drinks for the whole group.)

British pubs sell *draught*/AmE *draft* beer or lager (= from the barrel or keg) by the *pint*. (A British pint is rather more than half a litre; a US pint is smaller.) People ask for a *pint*, or a *half*. We do not usually say a *half pint*. Pubs sell spirits by the *measure*. If you want a large one, ask for a *double whisky* (etc.). They may then ask *What do you want in it? Neat* (adjective, or AmE *straight*) means with nothing added to it. *On the rocks* means with ice. Many pubs sell wine by the glass. *Soft* drinks are those without alcohol. When drinking with friends, the usual thing to say is *Cheers! Your health* is more formal.

(For the choice between *a drink* and *to drink*, see **verb or noun?**)

drop/fall/go down/cut/decrease/reduce/diminish/lessen

These words are all used about things that become, or are made, less.

1. *Drop, fall* and *go down* particularly mean 'get lower', of things that can be measured in that way:

drop: The price/the temperature/the wind/the speed has dropped (or *gone down*). *Sales/ numbers/profits/living standards/subscriptions have dropped* (or *gone down*). Except in a clear context, do not use *drop* in this sense as a transitive verb. To *drop prices* is clear, but to *drop military expenditure* will be taken to mean 'stop spending anything at all'.

fall: The price/the temperature/the level/oil consumption has fallen (or *gone down*). *Numbers/profits/living standards/subscriptions have fallen* (or *gone down*).

2. *Cut* is less formal than *decrease* and *reduce*. They all mean 'make (or get) less':

cut: To cut prices/costs/expenses/spending.

decrease: The price/the wind/the speed/the value/the amount has decreased. To decrease the price/the speed/oil consumption/wages.

reduce: To reduce taxes/the rent/the price/the subscription.

3. *Diminish* and *lessen* particularly mean 'make (or get) smaller'. They are not so much used of 'measureable' things:

diminish: The amount/his power/his strength has diminished.

lessen: To lessen the chances/the risk/the pain/the shock.

drown/sink

They both mean 'go down in water'. Air-breathing creatures *drown* or *are drowned* or *get drowned*. It means that they die in water: *Five people drowned/were drowned/got drowned.* Things, particularly ships, *sink* or *are sunk*. It means that they go to the bottom of water: *The boat sank/was sunk* (by a torpedo).

drunk/drunken

Drunk is the usual form after a verb: *He got drunk. You're drunk! Drunken* is normal before nouns: *drunken sailors. Drunken*, but not *drunk*, is used about states or events caused by drinking: *a drunken party* (but not **the party was drunk*). Note: *drunk(en) drivers/driving.*

dull/boring/tedious/troublesome/trying/tiresome

1. Things that are not interesting are *dull, boring* or *tedious: a dull* (or *boring* or *tedious*) *lecture, speaker, film, job, evening*. Things that cause problems and annoy you are *troublesome, trying* or *tiresome: a troublesome* (or *trying* or *tiresome*) *child, cough, experience.*

2. *Tiresome* does not mean 'tiring'. Compare:

a tiresome (= annoying) *child*

a tiring (= exhausting) *but delightful day*

each see both; singular or plural?

earliest

> TYPICAL MISTAKE: *Come and stay with us at the earliest!*

At the earliest means 'not before that time': *We won't get there till six at the earliest* (= not before 6). So the right thing to say would be *Come and stay with us at the earliest opportunity,* or *as soon as possible!*

earn see win(2)

economic/economical

Economic means either 'connected with finance' or 'profitable': *the government's economic policies; to charge an economic rent. Economical* means 'careful in using things without waste': *a more economical way of heating the house.*

either/also/too

> TYPICAL MISTAKES: *That isn't right, too. *I also don't know her.*

In negative sentences of this type, *either* replaces *too* and *also*: *'I can't drive.' 'I can't, either* (or *Neither can I*)!' (See also **both; neither.**)

elder

1. elder/older/elderly

Elder and *eldest* are used like *older, oldest* about someone's children, brothers, sisters, or cousins: *my elder* (or *older*) *sister* (= older than me); *the eldest* (or *oldest*) *of five sons.*

> *Elderly* means 'past middle age'. Compare:
>
> *his elder daughter* (= he has two daughters)
> *his elderly daughter* (= she is perhaps 65)

2. elder/major/minor/superior/inferior/senior/junior/preferable

> TYPICAL MISTAKES: *Luke is elder than Paul. *Our lettuces are more superior than yours.

These words are not true comparatives, though they may look like that. None of them can be used with *more* or *most*, or with *than* (though you can use *most* when it means 'very': *a most superior secretary*). To compare ages, say *Luke is older than Paul*.

Major and *minor* are not used in comparisons at all, and usually occur only before nouns: *He had a very minor operation*.

Superior, inferior, senior, junior and *preferable* are used with *to*. Although you cannot use *more, most* here, you can use words like *rather, somewhat, greatly, slightly*:

Our lettuces are superior to yours.
This hotel is much inferior to the one across the road.

(See also **prefer**; **word and preposition**.)

eminent see **famous**

employment see **work**

end

1. | TYPICAL MISTAKE: *At the end the bus arrived.

Do not confuse *in the end* with *at the end*, which means 'at the latest point': *at the end of the film/of 1993*.

2. in the end/at last/finally/lastly/in conclusion

In the end, at last and *finally* all describe what happened after a period of time, or perhaps as the result of a series of events: *We waited for hours, and in the end/at last/ finally the bus arrived*.

At last is used for good things rather than for bad things: *She was very ill, and in the end/finally* (not *at last*) *she died*. For the last thing in a series of actions, use *finally* or *lastly*: *Finally/Lastly, he dismantled the machine* (= after assembling it, demonstrating it, etc.).

To make the last point in a speech, use *finally, lastly*, or *in conclusion*: *And finally/ lastly/in conclusion, I should like to thank the domestic staff for all their help*. (Compare **first**.)

3. end/finish/stop (verbs)

They can all mean 'bring an activity to an end': *What time do you finish* (or, less formally, *stop*) *work?* (we do not **end work*). *Finish* is much commoner in this sense than *end*. To *end* an activity is to terminate it finally: *to end a discussion/a hunger strike*. To *finish* a task is usually to 'complete' it: *to finish a building/a university course*. You can *stop* an activity without *finishing* it. Compare:

> *She stopped reading the book* (= she was halfway through).
> *She finished (reading) the book* (= she reached the end).

endure see **stand**

engineering see **technology**

enter

> TYPICAL MISTAKES: **We entered into the theatre. *The Danube then enters into Austria.*

To *enter* a place is to go into it: *to enter the theatre/Austria*. We also *enter* a competition, an occupation, or an institution: *to enter a race/the university/politics/ Parliament*. You can *enter* something *for* a competition: *Her publishers have entered her latest novel for the Bloomsbury Prize*. (See also **exams**.)

entire see **all**

-er

This ending is joined onto a verb to make a noun for the person (or sometimes the thing) that does the action. *Diners* are people dining. But if you call someone a *dancer* or a *footballer*, it usually means that they do it as a profession. You can, however, say that someone is a *good dancer* or (BrE) a *keen footballer* when it is just a hobby.

especially see **specially(1)**

-ess see **feminine forms**

even

1. even though/if

Even though (not **even although*) is used like *though*, for talking about things that are (or perhaps will be) really true or really false: *It's hard work, but I enjoy it. (Even) though it's/it may be hard work, I enjoy/shall enjoy it* (here, *even* just adds a bit more 'surprise').

Even if means 'no matter if'. It is used, like *if*, for talking about things that may or may not be true. But compare:

> *If I could afford it, I'd go.*
> *Even if I could afford it, I wouldn't go.*

2. even/only

Compare:

> *He goes there only in winter* (= and not in summer).
> *He goes there even in winter* (= so certainly in summer).

These two meanings are quite easily distinguished. But sometimes the two words seem close in meaning. There are sentences where *even* means 'as much as', and *only* means 'as little as'. Compare:

> *He can't have read it even once!* (= he hasn't read it at all).
> *He can't have read it only once!* (= he must have read it more than once).

(For the position of *even* in sentences, see **word order**.)

eventual see **false friends**

every

We use *every* to talk about frequency: *I go there every Saturday. Every other* and *every second* mean 'each alternate': *Take the medicine every other day* (= on Monday, Wednesday, Friday . . .).

(For sentences like *Every child must bring his* (or *their*) *own lunch*, see **singular or plural? 3(b)**.)

everyone see **one(4)**

exams

You *enter for* an exam (formal *examination*), and then you *take* (or (BrE) *sit*, or (informally) *do*) it. You can *pass* or *fail* an exam or a test: *What year did you take your A levels? Has she passed her driving test?* (See also **undergo**.)

expect

If you *expect* something *to* happen, you think it will happen: *Nobody expects the fine weather to last* (or *expects that it will last*). But if you *expect* somebody *to do* something, you require them to do it as a duty. Compare:

> *I expect him to work hard* (= it's his duty).
> *I expect he will work hard* (= I think he will).

explain

TYPICAL MISTAKE: *She explained me the problem.*

Explain is not a verb like *give* (see **verb patterns(6)**). You *explain* things *to* people, but you do not *explain* people things: *She explained the problem to me.*

fabric see **cloth**

face/look/overlook

They can all mean the same thing: *Have you got a room facing/looking onto/overlooking the sea?* But *face* and *look* can be used for directions: *The room looks east. The seats face backwards.* (See also **look**.)

Overlook is for views from above: *Our neighbours' bedroom overlooks our garden.*

fairly see **quite(1b, 3)**

fall see **drop**

false friends

When words of similar form have the same meaning in more than one language, they are true friends to the language learner. Examples are German *Butter, Hand* and English *butter, hand*; *université* (French), *universidad* (Spanish), *università* (Italian), *Universität* (German), *uniwersytet* (Polish), *university* (English).

When words of similar form have very different meanings in more than one language, they seem to cause no problem for the language learner. Examples are German *Gift* (poison) and *Mist* (dung), which German-speaking learners of English do not confuse with English *gift* and *mist*.

But sometimes words in more than one language are similar in form and closely related but not identical in meaning. These are 'false' (deceitful) friends to the language learner, who may assume they are used in a second language as they are used in his own. False friends are of several types.

The best-known type is cognates that have developed differently in different languages. For example, German *müssen* and English *must* are related, and are often used alike, as are German *nicht* and English *not*. They can be true friends. Yet German *nicht müssen* means 'need not' or 'not have to', and so is not synonymous with English *must not*. (See **must**.) English *control* and French *contrôler* can also be true friends, but the French-speaking learner who says **The customs officer controlled my valise* will not be understood by English-speakers, who would use *inspected* here. Other well-known examples are *actual(ly)* and *eventual(ly)*. These are similar in form to *actuel(lement)* in French, *actual(mente)* in Spanish, etc., and to *éventuel(lement)* in French, *eventual(mente)* in Spanish, etc. But in English *actual* means 'real', whereas its cognates in other languages mean 'present or contemporary'; *eventual* means 'as the outcome' whereas its cognates mean 'possible'.

A second type of false friend is an English expression that has passed into another language and developed a different meaning there. The English word *shampooing*, which refers to a process, has passed into French as the name of the result of the process or of a substance used in the process: for both of these English uses *shampoo*. The English *veteran* has passed into Japanese, where it can mean 'expert'. But a Japanese who speaks of a *veteran lexicographer* will be interpreted as meaning an 'experienced' rather than an 'expert' one.

A third type is an expression from another language that has passed into English but is used differently here. Though French and English *menu* are often true friends, since they can both mean 'bill of fare', they can also be false friends, since French *menu* can also mean 'set meal' but English *menu* can't. The French expression *vis-à-vis de* has come into English without its *de* 'of', so we say *What is the government's position vis-à-vis taxation?*

A fourth type is an expression that has been coined in another language using English elements, but does not exist in English. Japanese *salaryman*, 'male office-worker or middle manager', was a prime example of this, but it has recently been taken up in English and may find a permanent home here.

A fifth type is a word in another language that is equivalent in meaning and deceptively similar in form, though such items are true friends to the language learner who remembers to adjust their form. Whereas English *questionnaire* and French *questionnaire* are friends as true as English *butter* and German *Butter*, English *millionaire (n)* and French *millionnaire (nn)* are not. A range of problems can be seen in these pairs of English and Spanish linguistic terms: *grammatical/gramatical; syntactic/sintáctico, -a; lexical/léxico, -a.* Each pair is essentially equivalent in meaning; but different enough in form to cause problems to the unwary.

The moral of the story is that if something in your language seems similar to something in English, make sure it really is similar before you use it in English or assume you understand its English counterpart.

familiar

> TYPICAL MISTAKE: *I try to be familiar with my pupils.*

When you know something, you are *familiar with* it, and it is *familiar to* you: *I am familiar with the neighbourhood. Her face is familiar to me.* But if you are *familiar with* a person, you treat them in too friendly a way, which is offensive: *Don't be so familiar!* Good teachers try to be *on friendly terms with* their pupils, and *familiar with* their problems, but never *familiar with* them.

famous/known/well-known/distinguished/eminent/ notorious/infamous

> TYPICAL MISTAKE: *The Costa Brava is a known tourist area.*

Known means 'clearly recognized': *a known blackmailer/cure for shingles.* You can, however, say *The Costa Brava is known/well known as a tourist area.*

Famous is like *well-known,* but stronger: *a famous actor/victory; a well-known local builder/restaurant.*

Distinguished and *eminent* are used of people who have worked in the professions: *a distinguished author/career; an eminent lawyer/doctor/statesman.*

Notorious means 'well-known for something bad': *the notorious murderer/scandal. Infamous* also means 'bad', but not always 'well-known': *infamous criminals/secret vices.*

far

1. far/a long way

> TYPICAL MISTAKE: *They live far (away) from the school.*

It is not strictly incorrect but unusual to use *far* with affirmative sentences. *Far* is used in questions and negatives about distance: *'Is it far?' 'No, it's not very far.'* It is also used in statements, after *as, too, so: It's much too far. We walked as far as the library. Tokyo is so far away!* Otherwise, use *a long way: They live a long way (away) from the school.*

2. far/distant

> TYPICAL MISTAKE: *Sheila is a far relation of mine.*

The chief uses of *far* as an adjective today are in expressions like *the far end of the shelf, the far side of the lake,* where it means the 'other' end or side; and in those like *the far Left, the far north of Norway,* where it means 'extreme'. We speak of *the far* (or *distant*) *future,* but only of *the distant past. Distant,* not *far,* is the word for 'not closely related': *Sheila is a distant relation of mine.* (See also **further/farther.**)

fasten/shut/do up/button up; open/unfasten/undo/unbutton

> TYPICAL MISTAKE: *Open the buttons of your coat!*

You *open* or *shut* (formal *close*) doors, windows, gates, boxes, drawers. *Fasten* is rather a general word for the act of tying, hooking, zipping, buttoning, buckling, clipping, or glueing anything: *Fasten your seat belts! Can you unfasten this knot? Unbutton* (or *Undo*) *your coat!* In the same way, you can *unhook* things with hooks, etc. (See also **put(2).**)

fatal

1. fatal/mortal/lethal

Fatal and (rather literary) *mortal* both mean 'resulting in death', and not merely 'serious': *a fatal/mortal disease, injury, blow; fatally/mortally wounded. Lethal* is used of the actual objects that kill you: *lethal chemicals, a lethal dose/weapon.*

Sometimes, however, *fatal* is used of something abstract that is very bad or inappropriate but need not cause death: *a fatal flaw in her character.* It can even be used humorously: *a fatal weakness for chocolates.* And *mortally offended* means 'gravely, seriously offended', though the outcome will probably not be death: *mortally offended by your refusal.*

2. fatal/fateful/fated

Fateful things are not necessarily 'fatal'. The word means 'having an important effect on the future', usually (but not always) disastrous: *a fateful decision/ announcement.* Something *fated* (to happen) seems inevitable, as if ordained by fate.

father/mother

These are the more formal words for parents: *Give my regards to your mother/father.* In speaking to one's brothers and sisters of one's own parents, this might be: *Give my love to Father/Mother. Daddy* and *mummy* (AmE *mommy*) are children's words: *Carry me, daddy!* Older sons and daughters may call their parents *dad* and *mum* (AmE *mom*). You might say *How's your dad?* but only to a friend.

feel see **adjective or adverb?**

feminine forms

The feminine ending *-ess* is correctly used for animals, and in female titles: *lioness; countess.* Otherwise, it is common today to speak of a woman as an *author*, a *poet*, a *manager*, or a *craftsman*, rather than an *authoress, poetess, manageress, craftswoman. Jewess* and *Negress* are impolite, though *actress, waitress* and *hostess* are still acceptable.

Often there is a neutral word we can use, such as *shop assistant* rather than *saleswoman.* (For the difference between *feminine* and *female*, see **masculine.**)

fetch see **bring**

fever see **countable and uncountable nouns**

few

1. few/a few; little/a little

> TYPICAL MISTAKES: *We invited them all, but a few came. *I've only got little time.

Few and *only a few* mean 'not many'. *A few* means 'some', when speaking of countables. *Little* and *only a little* mean 'not much'. *A little* means 'some', when speaking of uncountables. We never say *only few or *only little. Compare:

> *We invited them all, but few (or only a few) came.*
> *We invited them all, and a few actually came.*
> *I've only got a little time.*

(For *too few, too little*, see **short**.)

2. a few/a little/some

A few and *a little* suggest a smaller amount or quantity than *some*. Compare:

> *Can you spare me a few minutes?* (= not long).
> *You'd better sit down – it may take some minutes* (= a fairly long time).

Usually we cannot say *only some: *There were only a few* (not *only some) *cars in the street.* But if a customs officer asked what was in your suitcase, you might say *Only some souvenirs.* This means 'Nothing but souvenirs'. And *only some* can mean 'not all': *Only SOME insects are harmful.*

fewer/less

1. Correctly, *fewer* is used for plurals and *less* for uncountables: *fewer people; less water.* You will hear some people say, for instance, *?less people,* but this is not thought to be such good English. *More* is the opposite of both words: *more people/ water.*

2. In certain cases, however, we use *less* where one might expect *fewer*. When sums of money, distances, or periods of time are thought of as a 'quantity' rather than as a 'number', they take a singular verb. We then use *less: 5 years is* (not *are) a short time. He qualified in less than 5 years.* (See also **numbers(2)**.)

3. You can say *rather/somewhat/still/even/far/considerably/no/a lot fewer,* or *less: rather fewer flowers; even less weight.* But compare:

> *many fewer jokes*
> *much/a bit/a little less time*

Avoid the awkward combination *?a few fewer.* Say *a few less,* or *10 fewer students,* or *10 students fewer.* You can also say *one student fewer,* to avoid the awkward choice between *one fewer student* and *one fewer students,* which both sound odd. But note such phrases as *a number less than one* (e.g. .25).

fill

1. To put someone into a job is to *fill* it, not **fill it up*: *I'm afraid the vacancy's already been filled. Anne's the best person to fill this post.* (See **up.**)

2. fill in/up/out

When the British complete a form, they *fill* it *in*, or sometimes *up*; Americans *fill* it *in* or *out*: *I must fill in/*(BrE) *up/*(AmE) *out this application form.* Information is *filled in* on such a form: *Just fill in your name on this cheque.*

finally see end(2)

find

1. find/found

> TYPICAL MISTAKE: **I must found you somewhere to live.*

The two verbs are: *find, found, found* (= discover); *found, founded, founded* (= establish):

> *I must find you somewhere to live* (= discover).
> *She found me somewhere to live* (= discovered).
> *They decided to found a college* (= establish).
> *The college was founded in 1875* (= established).

2. find/find out

You *find out* facts, which means that you discover them by making an effort: *to find out the train times/the truth.* Otherwise, use *find*: *to find a solution to a problem.*

3. | TYPICAL MISTAKE: **I found the job interest me.*

When *find* means 'become aware of' something, or 'observe' it, it is used in these patterns:

> *I found that everyone had left.*
> *I find the job (to be) quite a challenge.*
> *I found her (to be/to have been) extremely helpful.*
> *I find it impossible to blame them.*
> *I found myself wondering what she meant.*
> *When I woke up, I found myself in hospital.*

The only infinitive verb that is used at all commonly with *find* is *to be*: *I found the job (to be) interesting.*

finish

1. finished/ready

Finished means 'ended, done'. *Ready* means 'prepared for use or action'. Compare:

> *Breakfast is ready* (= it's on the table to be eaten).
> *Breakfast is finished* (= we've eaten it all).

2. finish/finish with

> TYPICAL MISTAKE: *Have you finished with that poem you were writing?*

When you *have* (or *are*) *finished with* something or someone, you have no more use for them: *Can I use the typewriter when you've/you're finished with it?* Otherwise, use *finish*: *Have you finished that poem you were writing?* (See **end(3)**.)

first/at first/firstly

First can mean 'before anyone or anything else': *the first woman in space; the first time I'd been there* (= I'd never been before).

First can also mean 'at the beginning' of a period of time, in contrast with a later time. You can use *at first* with the same meaning: *When we first came to live here I didn't like it. I didn't like it at first.*

First and *firstly*, but not *at first*, are used for introducing a series of points you want to make: *First* (or *Firstly, First of all, In the first place), I'd like to thank you all for inviting me to speak.* (Compare **end(2)**.)

fix see repair

flight see journey

floor

1. floor/ground

> TYPICAL MISTAKE: *She was sitting on the ground in the kitchen.*

Indoors, the surface we walk on is the *floor*. The *ground* is out of doors: *to wash the kitchen floor*.

2. floor/storey

A *floor* or *storey* (AmE usually *story*) is a level of a building, with all the rooms that are in it: *an office on the third floor; a 100-storey skyscraper*. In AmE, the bottom floor at street level is called the *ground floor* or the *first floor*, and the next one above it is the *second floor*, and so on. In BrE, and sometimes in AmE, the bottom is the *ground floor* and the next above it is the *first floor*.

for

The problems here are over the choice between *for* and other prepositions.

1. with points of time

We use *at, in, on* here. But *for* can also be used with 'time' words, when we celebrate an occasion. Compare:

> *I bought him a boat on his birthday* (= that was the day I bought it).
> *I bought him a boat for his birthday* (= that was his present. I probably bought it earlier).

2. with lengths of time

When *for* means 'throughout the whole course of' a length of time, you can either use it or leave it out: *We waited (for) a long time.*

But with negatives, superlatives, *first* and *only*, *for* can mean 'at any time during' a length of time. Here, AmE speakers often use *in*: *It's the worst accident for* (esp. AmE *in*) *years*.

3. with destinations

You can often use either *for* or *to*: *I bought a ticket for/to Oxford.* Sometimes *for*, like *towards*, emphasizes the direction, and *to* the final destination. Compare:

> *We headed for Oxford* (= towards Oxford).
> *We drove to Oxford* (= we reached it).

(For the choice between *for* and *to* about 'purpose', see **to**. For the choice between *for* and *of* in names, see **of(4)**. See also **since(1); word and preposition**.)

forget

1.
> TYPICAL MISTAKE: **I've forgotten my book at home.*

Forget can mean 'not remember to bring or do something': *Don't forget your umbrella* (= take it with you). *Forget* is never used with expressions of place, such as *at home*. To let something remain somewhere, either by accident or on purpose, is to *leave* it there: *I've left my book at home. I've forgotten (to bring) my book.*

2. *Forget* can be followed, as a transitive verb, by a noun phrase, a *to-* infinitive, or an *-ing* verb. The rules are like those for *remember* (see **remember(1)**).

fortnight

This is a British word, as in *for a fortnight* and *once a fortnight*. Many Americans are familiar with such expressions, but prefer *for two weeks* and *every other week*, which the British understand but are less likely to use. The British *a fortnight's holiday* is for Americans *a two-week vacation*. A *fortnightly* meeting is held once every fortnight.

free

1. free/vacant/spare/leisure

If nobody is using a hotel room or a restaurant table, it is *free* or (more formal) *vacant*. The opposite is *occupied* or *taken*. We also speak of the *spare room* in a house, kept for visitors.

Time when you have nothing particular to do is *free, spare*, or (more formal) *leisure* time. Teachers and students in a school speak of a *free period*, when they are not teaching or being taught.

2. *Free* can be used like an adverb in certain phrases: *Let the rope run free*. But the usual adverb is *freely*. Only *(for) free*, not *freely*, can mean 'without payment'. Compare:

The children are educated (for) free (= nobody has to pay).
The children are freely educated (= at a permissive school).

(See also **adjective or adverb?**)

friendly

1. | TYPICAL MISTAKE: *She behaved very friendly.*

Friendly is an adjective. The related adverb would be *friendlily*, but that looks and sounds so odd that it is better to say *in a friendly way*.

2. When people are each other's friends, they are *friendly with* each other: *I'm getting quite friendly with our bank manager*. To be *friendly to* or *towards* someone is to treat them in a kind, pleasant way, as if you would like to be their friend: *Everyone was very friendly to us when we first came to live here*. (See also **pleasant**.)

frightful see awful

front

TYPICAL MISTAKE: *There was a big lorry at the front of us.*

At (or *in*) *the front of* something means 'in the front part of' it, so you can say *We sat at the front of the bus*. But when two things are separate, we speak of sitting *in front of* the television, or a lorry *in front of* us if we are driving.

frontier see **border**

fruit see **countable and uncountable nouns**

furious see **angry**

further/farther

You can say *I'm too tired to walk any further* (or *farther*), because both words can be used about distance in space or time: *The farther/further back we go in history, the less we know*. Only *further* is used in an abstract sense, or as a verb: *closed until further notice; to further his career*. *Farthest* and *furthest* are synonyms: *Who can jump the farthest/furthest?* It is not wrong to use *further, furthest* all the time.

fuss see **countable and uncountable nouns**

future tense

1. | TYPICAL MISTAKE: **I'll tell him when he will come home.*

We are traditionally taught not to use a future tense in these clauses, and this is usually good advice. The correct form is: *I'll tell him when* (or *as soon as*) *he comes home*. But the following are perfectly good English:

> *I wonder when he will come home?*
> *I won't give him the money unless he will* (= is willing to) *promise to pay it back.*

(For the future tense after *if*, see **conditionals(1)**.)

2. which 'future tense'?

English verbs have really only a 'present' tense, such as *is* and *go*, and a 'past' tense, such as *was* and *went*. There is no obvious 'future' tense corresponding to these. We have to choose between *will/shall*, *going to*, and the present tenses.

(a) We use the simple present tense about permanent facts which will still be true in the future: *When does the train leave? When do we get to Dover?* These are questions about the timetable, a permanent fact.

We use the simple present about dates: *Next Saturday is my birthday* (but *John will be eleven next Saturday*).

(b) When we speak of a future happening where there is no question of human 'willingness', we usually use *going to* or *about to* for what has all but started and may be too late to stop: *It's going to/about to rain; I'm going to/about to be sick!*

With a human subject, the negative *not about to* has become an informal expression of unwillingness: *I'm not about to work for free!*

But very often we want to speak about people's plans for the future, and then there are six choices. They range from the most 'fixed arrangement' to the most 'sudden decision':

I leave tomorrow.
I'm to leave tomorrow.
I'm leaving tomorrow.
I'll be leaving tomorrow.
I'm going to leave tomorrow.
I'll leave tomorrow!

For the difference between *be . . . -ing* and *going to*, compare:

How long are you staying? (= a question about your hotel booking).
How long will you be staying? (= a question about both your booking and your plans).
How long are you going to stay? (= a question about your plans).

The *will/shall* future is for personal decisions, rather than plans. Compare:

They aren't going to play (= there is no plan).
They won't play (= they refuse to).

The future continuous is neutral as between personal decisions and pre-arranged plans. So it can express discreet, noncommittal politeness in statements and questions: *They won't be playing* (= either because there is no plan or because they refuse to).

Avoid the combination *going to go*, which is considered to be bad style: *When are you going (to go) to the theatre?*

3. hope

The verb *hope* is used with either present or future, when there is no question of human 'willingness': *I hope it snows/will snow tomorrow.* When human willingness is involved, you must use the future: *I hope you'll visit us* (= an invitation).

gain see **win(2)**

game

A *play* is a drama performed by actors. *Play* (uncountable) is the activity of playing games: *Rain stopped play.* You *play* games, but *do* sports, though people sometimes say (esp. BrE) *play sport* with reference to games. A *game* is competitive, and need not be physical: *a game of tennis/chess/cards.*

A *sport* is physical, and need not be competitive. The word includes physical games such as football, and also swimming, riding and rock-climbing. An important public game or sports event is a *match* in BrE, though Americans prefer *game* here, too, except for board games: *a chess match; to play in a hockey match/game.*

get

1. get in/on, etc.

You *get on* or *onto*, and later *get off* a bicycle or a horse. You *get in* or *into*, and later *get out of* a car or a small boat. *Get on(to)* and *get off* can be used also about a bus, train, ship, or plane. BrE also uses *get out of* for trains and buses. To reach a place is to *get to* it, but we might ask *How do I get onto the motorway* BrE/(esp. AmE) *highway?* if we are driving along a side road.

2. TYPICAL MISTAKE: *Try to get the car starting.*

Get can mean 'cause to be in a certain state'. It is then used with adjectives, and with *-ed* participles: *to get the car started; to get a girl pregnant.* When this pattern is used with verbs, it refers to the result, and means 'so that it has been started, so that she is pregnant', etc.

Get can also mean 'cause to begin doing something'. It is then used with *-ing* participles: *to get the car going.* This pattern is used with 'activity' verbs, like *eat, work, run, write, speak.* It means 'so that it is working, so that they are speaking', etc.

Get means also 'persuade or cause to do something'. It is then used with the *to-*

infinitive, and suggests that there is some difficulty to be overcome: *to get the car to start.*

3. | TYPICAL MISTAKE: **He always gets dressed in national costume.*

When *get* is used with *-ed* participles, it usually becomes a sort of passive. To *get shot* or *get killed* is the same as to be shot or killed; to *get lost* or *get trapped* is to become lost or trapped.

But with certain verbs, *get* + *-ed* has the same meaning as the active, rather than the passive. Although to *get killed* is certainly not the same as to *kill*, to *get drowned* (or *be drowned*) is the same as intransitive to *drown* (= die under water). In the same way, to *change* (your clothes) is to *get changed*, and to *dress* (= put on clothes) is to *get dressed*. But note that *get dressed* means 'put on' clothes, not simply 'wear' them. Compare:

> *I'll come in a minute – I'm dressing* (or *getting dressed*).
> *He always dresses* (not **gets dressed*) *in national costume.*

(See also **linking verbs**.)

4. The principal parts of *get* are *get, got, got*. AmE also uses *gotten* usually as the past participle of *get*, 'receive, obtain', and often as that of *get*, 'become': *They've gotten many compliments on their latest book. They've gotten bigger since then.* BrE has *They've got* here. But AmE, like BrE, uses *got* as the past participle in the expressions *have got*, 'have, possess', and *have got to*, 'have to': *'I've got a lovely bunch of coconuts'* (old popular song); *I'm sorry: I've got to be going now.*

5. AmE also has *get to* = 'manage to', whose form with the past participle is *gotten to*. It can thus distinguish:

> *I've gotten to* (= I've managed to) *go there.*
> *I've got to* (= I have to) *go there.*

BrE does not readily use *get to* = 'manage to'. So in BrE the pair above would be:

> *I've managed to go there* (also possible in AmE).
> *I've got to go there.*

(See also **have(1, 3)**.)

girl see **woman**

go

1. This is perhaps the verb most commonly used with *and* instead of *to* to mean 'in order to': *I went and saw him. And* is, however, used with a number of other verbs:

Come and have tea with us. Wait and see. When you have to choose between *and* and *to*, these are the considerations:

(a) *And* is always less formal than *to*.
(b) *And* implies success. Compare:

> *I went and saw him and we talked about fishing.*
> *I went to see him but he was out.*

(c) Combinations such as *going and seeing, coming and having, been and seen* sound clumsy. *To try to do* something sounds clumsy in BrE, but not in AmE. Prefer: *I'm going to see him tomorrow. I've been to see her. I want to try and amuse them.*
(d) *Try and* is not used in the forms **tries and, *trying and, *tried and: He tries to leave* (not **tries and leaves*). *I'm trying to find out* (not **and finding out*). *He tried to stop her* (not **tried and stopped her*).

2. For *go down*, see **drop**. For *go mushrooming*, etc., see **-ing(3)**. For *going to*, see **future tense**. For *go mad*, etc., see **linking verbs**.

goal see aim

goodbye

Some informal ways of saying goodbye are *See you, Be seeing you, Bye, Bye-bye* and (BrE) *Cheers* or *Cheerio. Good day* is used at both meeting and parting in Australian English, but it is very formal and old-fashioned in both British and American use. *Good morning! Good afternoon!* and *Good evening!* (or just *Morning! Afternoon! Evening!*) are used for both meeting and parting at appropriate times of day, and can be addressed to strangers; but *Good night* is only for parting. (See also **greetings**.)

grass see countable and uncountable nouns

grateful see thankful

great see big

greetings

When you are formally introduced to a stranger, the thing to say is *How do you do?* and the answer is also *How do you do? Hello* is less formal, and used not only in introductions but when meeting a friend at any time. It is used at the beginning of a telephone conversation, by both speakers (see **telephone**). *Hi!* is even more informal. (See also **goodbye**.)

ground see **floor**

grow see **linking verbs; up(1)**

guest see **patient**

habit/custom/practice

A *habit* is something a person does regularly, and often unconsciously: *It's a bad habit to bite your nails.*

A *custom* is something that a whole society does regularly: *the custom of wearing black clothes at funerals.*

A *practice* is done by either an individual or a society. The word implies that it is done by choice, and often has a bad sense: *the practice of torturing prisoners.*

hair see **countable and uncountable nouns**

half

1. TYPICAL MISTAKE: **She swallowed half glass.*

You can say either *half a glass* or (particularly in AmE) *a half glass*, but such expressions must include *a/an*: *half an hour; half a mile.*

2. It is probably commoner to say *a month and a half, an hour and three quarters* than *one and a half months, one and three quarter hours.* Prefer *a* (rather than *one*) *month and a half* (see **a and the(3)**). But for numbers greater than one, we usually say, for example, *two and a half miles/weeks.*

(For *half was/were*, see **singular or plural?(3)**. See also **drinking**.)

hand

TYPICAL MISTAKE: **Peter isn't clever; on the other hand, he's rather stupid.*

On the other hand means 'however'. It is used for adding something new that does not actually contradict a statement: *Peter isn't clever; on the other hand, he's very friendly and helpful.*

On the contrary is used for contradictions: *Peter isn't clever; on the contrary, he's rather stupid. In contrast to* or *by contrast with* shows the surprising difference between two facts that are both true: *Peter isn't clever; by contrast, his little brother is brilliant.*

happen/occur/take place/arise/crop up/break out/emerge/transpire/eventuate

TYPICAL MISTAKE: *A misunderstanding took place.*

Events *happen*, or (more formally) *occur*, usually by accident and without planning: *The explosion/tragedy happened last week. Many changes have occurred in my lifetime.*

Events *take place*, usually by arrangement: *When will the wedding take place?*

Things that *arise*, or (informally) *crop up*, begin unexpectedly to exist: *A misunderstanding arose.*

When bad things begin suddenly, they *break out*: *War/Fire/Panic/Disease/Fighting broke out.*

To *emerge*, or (more formal) *transpire*, is to become known after being hidden: *The truth finally emerged. It transpired that they were both heroin addicts.*

To *eventuate* (rare and formal) is to happen as a result: *If the interest rate rises, mass unemployment will eventuate.*

hardly

1. *Hardly, scarcely* and *barely* are correctly followed by *when*: *I had hardly opened the door when the dog bit me.* (You will hear people say *hardly ... than*, but this is not thought to be good English.) On the other hand, *no sooner* is followed by *than*: *I had no sooner opened the door than the dog bit me.* (See also **inversion(2)**.)

2. *Hardly* means 'almost not', so do not confuse it with the adverb *hard*. People *work hard*, not **hardly*, and we speak of *hard-earned* money and *hard-boiled* eggs. Compare:

The company was hard hit by the oil crisis (= they suffered loss).
The company was hardly hit by the oil crisis (= they were almost unaffected).

3. TYPICAL MISTAKE: **There's hardly room for something else.*

Hardly, scarcely and *barely* are like negatives, so where there is a choice they must be used with *any, anything*, etc., rather than with *some, something*: *There's hardly room for anything else.* (See also **can/could(1a)**.)

hate see ²like(2)

have

1. have/have got

When *have* means 'possess', it is used with or without *got. Have got* is acceptable everywhere; *had got* is much more likely in BrE than in AmE:

I've got three sons; (AmE, or formal BrE) *I have three sons.*
I haven't got/I don't have any sons; I've got no sons; (formal) *I have no sons.*
Had/Hadn't she got/Did/Didn't she have black hair?

The things to remember are:

(a) The following negative and question forms are nowadays very formal: *He hasn't a beard. Has he a beard?* Use the *have got* form or the *do have* form, unless some other word comes between *have* and the noun, like *enough* here: *I haven't (got) enough money.*
(b) The short forms *-'s, -'ve, -'d* are used before *got* except in formal writing, where you may prefer to use *have* alone: *I've got/I have a cat. They'd got/They had lots of money.*

2. When *have* means 'receive', 'obtain', 'cause', or 'experience', it is not used with *got* (see also **to(2)**): *Do you have sugar in your tea? I had a bad cold last week.* But compare:

Had they got enough to eat? (= did they possess it?)
Did they have enough to eat? (= did they possess it OR did they receive it?)

3. have (got) to

I (do) have to and *I've got to* both mean 'I must'. Again, BrE prefers the form with *got:*
I haven't got to = I don't have to. The *got* form is less common in the past tense, and does not exist in the future or with the modal verbs: *I had to/I didn't have to. I'll/I won't/I may have to.* The things to remember are:

(a) Avoid the forms *?I haven't to go; ?Have you to go?* They are not standard English.
(b) Word order is important. A noun between *have* and *to* changes the meaning. Compare:

He has to drink lots of milk (= he must).
He has lots of milk to drink (= he's got plenty).

(See also **must; need**. For *gotten*, see **get(4,5)**.)

he or she

1. English has no singular pronoun referring to both sexes in the way that *they* refers to the plural. In former times, *he, his, him* were used unthinkingly for both: *Each member must clean his own room.* But nowadays, many people prefer to make it clear that women as well as men are included. There are several ways of doing this:

(a) You can use *he or she,* or *he/she: Each member must clean his or her* (or *his/her*) *own room.*
(b) You can turn it into the plural, or use other pronoun forms: *All members must clean their own rooms. Each of us must clean our own room* and even *Each of them must clean their own room.*

(c) Except in very formal writing, it is now common (as in this book) to use *they, their, them*, particularly after *anybody, everybody, somebody, nobody*: *Somebody's left their coat behind!* Remember that there is nothing wrong with using *he*, etc., about an all-male group, or *she*, etc., about an all-female group: *Every member of the fraternity must clean his own room. Every member of the sorority must clean her own room.*

2. Anything that is not a person is usually referred to as *it*. This includes animals, though we may use *he* or *she* about a pet animal. It even includes babies, though it is more polite to say *he* or *she* when talking to the baby's parents. Ships are *she*, and some people use *she* of their car. It is not wrong, though rather old-fashioned, to use *she* about countries, and the moon is often *she* in poetry. But there it stops; the *government*, for instance, is *it*.

Animals that are *he* or *she* are *who/that*; inanimates that are *she* (or *he*) are *which/that*: *a dog who/that has lost his bone* (or *a dog which/that has lost its bone*); *a ship which/that has lost her/its bearings.*

head/chief/director/manager/boss

These are words for a person in authority, the highest official. *Head* is used particularly, though not only, in education, so that we speak of the *head* of a school or of its history department, but a monarch is a *head of state*. *Chief* seems to be preferred in government and the police. Both these words are used in certain combinations: *head teacher; head waiter; head gardener; chief constable; chief justice; chief librarian*.

A *director* may be in charge of a government organization, or one of the *board of directors* who manage a company. The word is used in connection with the arts, so that we speak of a *film director*, and of the *artistic director* of an opera company. (The principal first violinist of a symphony orchestra is called the *leader* of the orchestra in BrE, but the *concertmaster* in AmE.)

A *manager* is an employee, not an owner, of a business enterprise. We speak of a *bank manager*, or the *manager* of a hotel or restaurant. A *theatre manager* handles the finances of the theatre.

Boss is an informal word for an employer, who gives one orders.

healthy/wholesome

TYPICAL MISTAKES: *She was soon healthy again. *It's a very wholesome climate.*

Healthy people are physically strong, not merely 'not ill'. Someone who has recovered from an illness is *well*, or *better* (see **sick(3)**): *She was soon well again*. The outward signs of health are called *healthy*, and so are things that are physically good for you: *a healthy appetite; a healthy climate. Wholesome* is used particularly of food: *a wholesome diet*. Both words can be used figuratively: *a healthy/wholesome disrespect for authority.*

hear

1. hear/listen

> TYPICAL MISTAKE: *I was hearing a symphony.*

To *hear* a sound is to take it in with your ears. To *listen to* it is to pay attention to it. In this sense, *hear* is not used in the *-ing* form: *I was listening to a symphony.* (See **simple or continuous?**)

2. hear/learn

Both words can mean 'become informed of something': *I'm sorry to hear/*(more formal) *learn that she's failed.* But if you have *heard of* something, you know of its existence: *He's never heard of Aristotle.* To *hear about* something is to receive news about it: *Did you hear about what happened at the wedding?* (See **word and preposition**.)

help

> TYPICAL MISTAKE: *The movement helped with awakening the people.*

If a person or organization is useful to someone by doing something, these are the patterns:

> *Can I help?*
> *I helped her (to) clean the house.*
> *I helped (her) with the cleaning.*
> *He helped in the reorganization of the school.*
> *Perhaps the local Council will help you.*

But if something contributes to a result, the only possible patterns are:

> *The movement helped (to) awaken the people.*
> *The finding of oil helped our economic growth.*
> *Some extra money would help.*

(For *help* as a noun, see **countable and uncountable nouns**. See also **serve**.)

high/highly

High, not *highly*, is used to show the 'result' of a verb: *He climbed high into the mountains.* (See **adjective or adverb?(1)**.) *Highly* is used like *very*, before adjectives and participles: *highly infectious; highly intelligent. Highly* can also mean 'very well': *highly paid; she spoke highly of your work.*

But certain compound nouns and adjectives use *high*: *high-flyer; high-grade; high-heeled* (shoes); *high-level* (talks); *high-powered* (executives); *high-tension* (wires). Here, we are saying that the heels, power, tension, etc., are *high.* Workers can be *high-paid* or *highly paid* (same meaning). (For the choice between *high* and *tall*, see **big**.)

historic/historical

> TYPICAL MISTAKE: *The Battle of Hastings was of great historic importance.*

Historic means 'memorable; important in history': *a historic occasion; historic buildings.* So *great historic importance* is like saying 'great important importance'.

Historical means 'about history': *historical research; historical novels.* So you can say *The battle was of great historical importance* (= very important in history). *Historical* also means 'having really existed in the past', or 'because of past events': *Was Robin Hood a historical character?*

holiday/vacation

A single day when one does not work is a *holiday*: *New Year's Day is a public holiday.* A longer period is a *holiday* (BrE) or a *vacation* (AmE): *I get four weeks' paid holiday/vacation.* When you are having a holiday you are *on holiday/vacation.* You can be on holiday without going away anywhere. Compare:

> *The house is noisy when the children are home on holiday/vacation.*
> *Our secretary is (away) on holiday/vacation this week* (= she's not here).

The plural *holidays* is also used in BrE, particularly by schoolchildren and teachers, as the opposite of 'termtime': *They went to France during the summer holidays/(AmE) vacation. Vacation* is only used in the plural when we speak of more than one such period: *He spends all his Christmas vacations skiing.* British universities and lawcourts, as well as American ones, use the word *vacation.*

home

The adverb *home*, not the phrase *at home*, is used with verbs of motion: *to go/come/arrive/hurry home; to bring/send the children home. Home* is also used like this with *be* and *get*, when they refer to 'arriving': *We'll soon be/get home.* It is correct to use *at home* to mean 'in one's house', where no motion is involved; but in both AmE and informal BrE, *at* is often omitted here, too: *to stay (at) home; she works/sleeps/lives at home.* If you are at home you are *in.* If you are not at home, you are *out.*

hope see **future tense(3)**; **wish(2)**

horrible see **awful**

hostage see **prisoner**

hotel see **restaurant(1)**

how see **what**

however see **nevertheless**

hurt

1. hurt/injured/wounded

> TYPICAL MISTAKE: *He was wounded in a car crash.*

People are *wounded* on purpose, in war or fighting and with bullets, knives, or swords. They are *hurt* or *injured* with other weapons such as sticks or bombs, or else in accidents: *He was injured in a car crash.* Both *wound* and *injure* are more serious than *hurt*.

2. hurt/offend

To *hurt* someone can mean to be unkind to them, to make them unhappy: *I didn't want to hurt you/to hurt your feelings.* To *offend* someone is to annoy and insult them: *You must be careful not to offend the customers.* Compare also:

> *I was rather/very/deeply hurt* (= in mind).
> *I was badly/seriously hurt* (= in body).

hyphens

1. There are no fixed rules about whether to write, for instance, *ice cream, ice-cream,* or *icecream*. Consult a dictionary. In general, the British seem to use hyphens more than the Americans, but the general tendency is for these noun-noun compounds to become fused into single words: *boyfriend; gasworks; weekend.* (This does not happen if there are more than two components, as in *daughter-in-law*.) But hyphens are used:

(a) when an 'open compound', or a whole phrase, is turned into an adjective before a noun. Compare:

> *They live next door; our next-door neighbours.*
> *They're 14 years old; 14-year-old boys* (Two hyphens here. *14 year-old boys* would be 14 boys who are each one year old!)

(b) in most combinations with *-ing, -er, -ed: hang-gliding; organ-grinder; left-handed.*
(c) in many noun-adjective combinations: *ice-cold; coal-black.*
(d) to join prefixes to words, particularly *ex-* and *non-*. Always use a hyphen before a capital letter: *ex-husband; non-alcoholic; un-American.*
(e) in numbers from twenty-one to ninety-nine: *twenty-two; thirty-first; five hundred and forty-seven; the year nineteen ninety-three.*
(f) where necessary, to avoid ambiguity. Compare:

> *to recover* (= get back) *consciousness; to re-cover* (= cover again) *the sofa.*
> *an Irish-whiskey* (= it is Irish) *manufacturer; an Irish* (= he is Irish) *whiskey-manufacturer.*

2. Hyphens are also used to divide words at line endings. Again, there are not many fixed rules, but the following are generally agreed:

(a) Do not divide single-syllable words: *leng-ths*.
(b) Do not leave fewer than three letters each side of the hyphen: *easi-ly; *be-fore*.
(c) If a word is already hyphenated, divide it there: *un-Ameri-can*.
(d) Divide 'solid' compounds at their point of joining: *tea-spoon*, not *teasp-oon*.
(e) Avoid divisions that leave something strange on one side or the other: *ear-nest* (= nothing to do with ears or nests!).
(f) Some dictionaries show syllable divisions. Of these, some show only where a word can be divided at the end of a line. Others, however, show all syllable boundaries, including those where a word should *not* be divided at the end of a line. When consulting a dictionary for syllable divisions, make sure you know what its policy is.

ice(d)

Very cold drinks are *iced*: *iced tea/beer/water* (the expression *ice water* is chiefly AmE). The British often call an ice cream an *ice*. The Americans do not, unless it is a 'water ice', without milk or cream. In BrE, an *ice lolly* (from *lollipop*) is a piece of water ice on a stick, similar to what Americans might call a *Popsicle* (trademark).

-ics

Nouns that end with *-ics*, such as *politics*, can take a singular or plural verb. They are singular when they mean a science, art, or academic subject; plural when they mean activities or properties. Compare:

> *Politics is the art of government. Her politics* (= political opinions) *are very odd.*
> *Acoustics is the study of sound. The acoustics of this theatre are very bad.*

ill see sick

in/into

1. With verbs about position, you must use *in*, not *into*: *She spent the morning in* (not **into*) *the kitchen*. With verbs of motion, you can use either *in* or *into*. *Into* is slightly more formal: *They went in/into the shop.*

In may be preferred to *into* when you are thinking of being surrounded by an area, rather than being inside a closed container: *Put the chairs in the garden*. But you must use *into* if it is important to distinguish 'movement' from 'position'. Compare:

> *Go down those steps into the garden* (= they lead there).
> *Go down those steps in the garden* (= they are there).

2. | TYPICAL MISTAKE: **3 into 12 is 36.* |

Into is used when dividing one number by another: *3 into 12 goes 4 times* (or *3 into 12 is 4*). It is not used in multiplication: *3 times 12 is 36.*

include see comprise

infamous see famous

inferior see elder(2)

inform

> TYPICAL MISTAKES: *I shall inform the details to them. *Please inform me the details.*

Inform is not a verb like *tell* (see **verb patterns(4d)**). You *inform* people *of* facts: *Please inform me of the details; When the films are developed I will inform you; He informed her that he was married already.*

-ing

1. to eat or eating?

If a verb follows certain verbs or phrases, it must be in the *-ing* form (the gerund or verbal noun). Here are some common ones:

acknowledge	*He acknowledged having* (not *to have) written the letter.
admit	*She admitted having* (not *to have) opened it.
avoid	*I can't avoid stepping* (not *to step) on them.
consider	*Would you consider buying* (not *to buy) a bicycle?
deny	*He denied having* (not *to have) taken the money.
enjoy	*They enjoy walking* (not *to walk).
fancy	*Fancy wearing* (not *to wear) a swimsuit in the snow!
finish	*I've finished painting* (not *to paint) it.
give up	*He gave up smoking* (not *to smoke).
can't help	*I can't help being* (not *to be) fat.
imagine	*Imagine living* (not *to live) in a castle!
keep on	*He kept on complaining* (not *to complain).
mind	*She doesn't mind being* (not *to be) asked.
miss	*You mustn't miss seeing* (not *to see) the film.
postpone	*We'll postpone selling* (not *to sell) the flat.
practise	*I practised steering* (not *to steer) the boat.
put off	*He put off answering* (not *to answer) the letter.
regret	*They regretted leaving* (not *to leave) France.
repent	*He repented having* (not *to have) said it.
resent	*She resents being* (not *to be) treated like that.
resist	*I couldn't resist telling* (not *to tell) her.
risk	*You mustn't risk losing* (not *to lose) it.
can't stand	*He can't stand being* (not *to be) laughed at.
suggest	*I suggest asking* (not *to ask) her.
no good/no use	*It's no good/no use arguing* (not *to argue).

After some verbs, a verb must be in the *to-* infinitive form. Some common ones are:

agree   choose   demand   long   promise
aim   claim   deserve   manage   refuse
arrange   consent determine mean   threaten
ask   decide   expect   offer   want
attempt   decline hope   pretend   wish

But often, you can use either form of the following verb: *He began dancing/to dance.* (See also **begin**.) Sometimes there is a slight difference of use or meaning:

(a) After *like, love, hate*, the Americans often use the *to-* infinitive where the British would prefer the *-ing* form: *He likes driving/to drive fast cars.* But both the Americans and the British use the *to-* infinitive, particularly after *would like/love/hate*, when speaking about preferences and wishes: *I'd love to go to Disneyland. I like* (= I prefer) *to arrive early at parties.*
(b) Compare:

> *He went on complaining* (= he didn't stop).
> *He went on to complain* (= he then complained).

(For some other verbs with this distinction, see **remember, stop.** See also **used to.**)

2. after a preposition

(a) Prepositions (*in, at, by,* etc.) are always used with a noun or nounlike word. If the noun is replaced by a verb the verb is always in the *-ing* form: *keen on tennis/ swimming; incapable of dishonesty/stealing.* (See **word and preposition**.)

(b) | TYPICAL MISTAKE: **I look forward to see you.*

The word *to* is used either as an ordinary preposition, or to introduce the *to-* infinitive. When it is an ordinary preposition it must be followed by *-ing*, and the test is whether the verb could be replaced by a noun: *I look forward to the party/seeing you.*
    In the following examples, *to* is an ordinary preposition:

> *a new approach to teaching* (not **teach*) *English.*
> *I object to being* (not **be*) *treated like that.*

(c) | TYPICAL MISTAKE: **I hurt myself at playing football.*

In some sentences, where the subject of the two verbs is the same, you can run them together. No preposition is needed: *I hurt myself playing* (= when I was playing) *football.*

3. Some verbs, particularly words for sports and hobbies, seem to exist only in the *-ing* form, often with an associated *-er* noun. We speak of *cinemagoing* (esp. BrE = AmE *moviegoing*) and a *cinemagoer* (esp. BrE = AmE *moviegoer*), but there is no verb **to cinemago*: *We went windsurfing/hang-gliding/sightseeing/mushrooming* (= picking mushrooms)*/blackberrying; the cricketing nations; a party of windsurfers/sightseers/ cricketers.* (See **-er.**) (The other forms of such verbs are, however, 'latent', and can be created when they are needed: *We windsurfed off the coast.*)

injure see hurt

intensifiers

These are adjectives and adverbs that 'intensify' other words, making them stronger. Many of them have a physical meaning (*strong man, deep hole*), but when you speak of abstract matters you must choose a suitable adjective to go with the noun, or adverb to go with the verb or adjective (for intensifiers of verbal adjectives, see **verbal adjectives(2)**). Here are some frequent combinations:

(a) *great, large, enormous, tremendous, terrific. Great* is often used with uncountable nouns that mean feelings and qualities: *great pride/admiration/skill.* When it is used with countable nouns, *great* is more formal than *big: a great/big surprise* (see **big**). *Greatly* is used with verbs, particularly *-ed* participles: *greatly improved/influenced.*
   Large is chiefly used of physical things, but also of numbers and quantities: *a large number/proportion/population.* (*Largely* is different. It means 'mostly': *Her success was largely due to her mother.*)
   Enormous, tremendous and (informal) *terrific* are stronger than *great: an enormous/ a tremendous amount of money; terrific speed; enormously rich.*
(b) *high, deep, heavy, strong, hard, extreme, intense. High* is used particularly of measurable things: *high speed/price/cost/level.* It can also mean 'very good': *high quality/opinion* (see **high/highly; big**).
   Deep emphasizes the seriousness of feelings and conditions: *deep trouble; deeply grateful.*
   Heavy emphasizes force, often in an alarming sense: *heavy fighting/casualties/ traffic; snowing heavily; heavily armed.*
   Strong is for things that have a powerful effect: *strong influence/criticism/opinions; I feel strongly about it; he strongly denied it.*
   Hard can mean 'tough and strenuous': *hard work/workers; to try hard.* (See **hardly**, which is different.)
   Extreme and *intense* are very much alike: *extreme/intense heat* (or cold); *extreme danger/poverty. Intense* is particularly used about feelings and experiences: *intense resentment.*
(c) *absolute, complete, total, utter, thorough.* These accompany nouns for very strong feelings and happenings: *absolute despair; a complete surprise; a total stranger; utter disregard; a thorough waste of time; absolutely ridiculous; completely successful.*
(d) *distinct, definite, marked.* These all mean 'clear and noticeable': *a distinct smell/*

improvement; a definite possibility; a marked resemblance; distinctly/definitely/markedly better; I distinctly (not **markedly*) *remember . . . .*

(e) *serious, bad, bitter.* These can all emphasize bad things: *a serious crime/injury/ problem; a bad cold/mistake. Bitter* is for feelings: *a bitter blow/disappointment; seriously* (or *badly*) *hurt/injured/wounded/damaged; seriously* (not **badly*) *ill; badly* (not **seriously*) *beaten/defeated* (see **hurt**).

(f) *fierce, heated, urgent, desperate. Fierce* implies energy: *a fierce argument; fierce competition/resistance, fiercely competitive. Heated* means 'angry and excited': *a heated argument/quarrel/discussion; argued heatedly* (compare *warm* at (g) below). *Urgent* or *desperate* situations must be dealt with quickly: *an urgent need for medical supplies.*

(g) *warm, hearty.* These can imply good feelings: *warm/hearty congratulations* (compare *heated* at (f) above); *She greeted them warmly.* But *heartily* just means 'thoroughly': *I heartily dislike him.*

interested

1. interested/interesting

> TYPICAL MISTAKE: **Are you interesting in astronomy?*

Things that interest people are *interesting,* and the people are *interested in* them: '*Are you interested in astronomy?*' '*Yes, it's an interesting subject.*' (See also **verbal adjectives**.)

2.
> TYPICAL MISTAKE: **I was interested in learning that she had sold the house.*

When you receive a particular bit of interesting news, the news is introduced by the *to-* infinitive, followed typically by a noun-phrase or clause. Compare:

I was interested (or *surprised, glad, sorry*) *to learn that she had sold the house.*
I was interested in learning to play the violin.
I'd be interested to know what happened.

3. All the following alternatives are good English: '*Is that true?*' *I asked, interested/ interestedly/with interest.* Except in really formal writing we now often form *-ly* adverbs from verbal adjectives. *Interestedly* is perhaps the most common.

interfere in/with

> TYPICAL MISTAKE: **The chiming of the clock interfered in the concert.*

If you *interfere in* a matter, or *between* people, you try to influence it or them when it is not your business: *Stop interfering in my affairs!* If something *interferes with* something else, it prevents it or spoils it: *The chiming of the clock interfered with the concert.* In BrE, to *interfere with* a child is to make illegal sexual approaches: *He was arrested for interfering with a little girl.*

interview

When you are interviewing someone you *hold* the interview, and the person *has* it. A famous person may *give* (or, more formally, *grant*) an interview to the press.

introductions

Here are some common phrases used when introducing people to each other:

'By the way, do you know each other? (or Have you met before?) Ron Evans, Jim Sinclair.' 'How do you do?' (See **greetings**.)
'I don't think we've met. I'm (or My name is) Susan Smith. I'm Peter's sister.' 'Hello (or Hi)! I'm Brian.' 'Hello!'
'Bill, this is (or I'd like you to meet) Mary Watkins.' 'How do you do?'
'Bill, do you know (or have you met) Mary Watkins?' 'No, I don't think so. How do you do?'

Correctly, a younger or less important person is introduced to an older or more important one: 'Archbishop, this is Susan Smith.' 'How do you do, Miss Smith?'

intrude see disturb

invade see conquer

invent/discover

> TYPICAL MISTAKE: *Columbus invented America.*

You *invent* (= make) things that did not exist before. You *discover* (= find) things that existed before but were not known. Compare:

Columbus discovered America.
Bell invented the telephone.

inversion

The normal English word order for statements is subject–verb–object–adverbs, etc. (See **word order**.) In questions the order is question word–verb–subject (or the subject between two parts of the verb):

John eats spaghetti.
Does John eat spaghetti?
What does John eat?

But there are various kinds of statement where the verb comes before the subject, as in a question.

1. In such combinations as *neither could I; nor is William; so must you*. The order **neither I could* is wrong. (See also **neither(5); nor**.)

2. When the sentence begins with *never, seldom, rarely, hardly, scarcely, barely, not only, no sooner,* and negative phrases such as *in no circumstances, in neither case, least of all*. This is a rather literary word order. Compare:

> *I've never met such an extraordinary man.*
> *Never have I met . . . .*
> *I had hardly/scarcely . . . .*
> *Hardly/Scarcely had I . . . .*

(For inversion after *only*, see **only**.)

3. In such combinations as: *Here comes the bride; There goes the postman* (but *Here she comes; There he goes*). These are normal. We often use the same pattern, though we need not, in sentences where *there* can be left out: *Next (there) came the soldiers. Out of this (there) developed a new theory.*

4. When a 'speech' verb follows direct speech: *'Yes,' said Mary/replied George*. This, too, is normal, but so is the other order: *'Yes,' Mary said*. Nowadays this other order is preferred with pronouns: *'Yes,' he replied.*

5. You will see subject–verb inversion used after *as* and *than*. This is a formal use, and there is no need to adopt it unless the subject is very long: *. . . than did the audience. . . . than did the predominantly middle-class audience.*

6. Another formal and rather old-fashioned pattern uses inversion instead of *if* in conditional sentences. Compare:

> *If it had been winter . . . .*   *If it were to/should rain . . . .*
> *Had it been winter . . . .*   *Were it to/should it rain . . . .*

invitations

In speech you might say:

> *Can you come to dinner on Thursday?*
> *Would you like to spend Sunday with us?*

The answer might be:

> *Thank you very much. I'd love to. That would be great!*
> *I'd love to/like to, but unfortunately . . . .*

In writing, it might be:

> *We are having a party at (time) on (date) to celebrate . . . and hope you will be able to join us.*

The answer might be:

> *Thank you for your very kind invitation. I am looking forward to it.*
> *It was very kind of you to invite me, but unfortunately . . . .*

it

1. *It* is used as the subject of sentences about the weather, time, or distance: *It's raining/cold/a lovely day. I hope it keeps fine. It's Thursday/lunch time/my birthday. It's not far/100 miles to Birmingham.*

2. *It* is often used in sentences where the real subject or object comes later. Compare:

> *Seeing myself on television felt funny.*
> *It felt funny seeing myself on television.*

In informal speech we often leave out *it* at the beginning of this second kind of sentence. This is not wrong: *(It) Doesn't matter! (It) Serves you right!*

3. *It* is also used, rather informally, as a dummy (direct) object to allow certain verbs to form complete predicates (verb phrases): *Beat it!* (esp. AmE); *The car broke down and I had to leg it back home.*

(For the choice between *it*, *he*, *she*, see **he or she**. For the choice between *it* and *that*, see **that(2).** See also **it's; there(4).**)

it's

1. it's/its

TYPICAL MISTAKE: ** The cat washed it's face.*

It's means either 'it is' or 'it has'. *Its* means 'of it'. Compare:

> *It's* (= it is) *ready.*
> *It's* (= it has) *eaten it.*
> *its face*

2. it's me

This is now standard idiomatic English, far more usual than the very formal *It is I*. We also say *That's me in the photograph.*

job see **work**

join

1. | TYPICAL MISTAKE: *He intends to join politics.*

People *join* a group when they become a member of it: *to join a queue/a club/the Labour Party.* We do not normally *join* places or occupations: *He intends to take up* (not **join) politics.*

2. join/link/connect/combine/unite

Join, link and (more formal) *connect* imply bringing things into a close relationship while preserving their separate identities: *Connect/Join the two points.* Often there is something intervening that joins them: *The canal links/connects the two oceans.* When they are used of abstract things, *link* suggests a closer relationship than *connect*: *His name was linked with the bombing.*

Combine and *unite* imply that the items become one whole: *to combine carbon with hydrogen. Unite* is used particularly of political units: *the United States of America.*

journey/trip/tour/voyage/cruise/flight/ride

A *journey* is from one place to another, and the word refers to the actual travelling: *to go on* (less commonly *make*) *a journey to/across/through a place; a long journey by car/ bus/train* (but *on foot*).

A *trip* is a journey to a place and back again, for business or pleasure; a 'visit': *a trip to/across/through/round/around* (not **of) a place; to go on a business trip to Tokyo/a coach* (BrE = AmE *bus*) *trip round the island.* Americans can also *take a trip*, for pleasure rather than business; they do not usually ?*take trips*.

A *tour* involves visiting several places: *to go on a tour round/around/of Europe; a walking/cycle tour.*

A *voyage* is a long sea journey. Like *journey*, the word refers to the actual travelling: *to go on a voyage to India/across the Pacific/through the Dardanelles.* A *cruise* is a tour by sea: *to go on a cruise round the Mediterranean.*

A *flight* is a journey by air, usually one scheduled on a commercial aircraft: *Flight BA 142 to Paris now boarding.*

Ride refers to the actual means of transport, and is used of short distances: *a ride on a camel; to go for a bike ride through Innsbruck* (= an hour or so). (See also **ride**.)

junior see **elder**

keep

1. keep/put

> TYPICAL MISTAKE: *I've kept the key on your ring.*

To *keep* something in a place is to have it always there. To move something into a place is to *put* it there. Compare:

> *I've put* (= fixed, fastened) *the key on your ring.*
> *I keep* (= store) *the tapes in this cupboard.*

2. keep (up)

> TYPICAL MISTAKE: *He never keeps up his promises.*

We *keep* (= fulfil) promises and appointments. We *keep up* (= not allow to stop) traditions, standards, contacts, payments. (See **up**.)

kind see **sort**

knit/knitted

Use the past form *knitted*, except when the participle forms part of a compound adjective: *She knitted some socks; a knitted scarf; he knitted his brows* (= frowned); *a chunky-knit sweater; a close(ly)-knit family.*

know

> TYPICAL MISTAKES: *She knows to drive. *She knows driving.*

Know in the sense of 'have the necessary skill' is not followed by *-ing*, or by the *to-* infinitive alone. If you need to use the *to-* infinitive it must be introduced by *how*: *She knows how to drive* (or, more commonly, *She can drive*). You may hear people say things like *She knows to lock the door*, with a *to-* infinitive, but this is different. It means that she knows she must do it, and that she is sensible enough to do it.

In the sense of 'have a fact in your mind', *know* is used either alone, or with *of* or *about*, or with an object or a clause. The patterns are:

> *Yes, I know!*
> *I know her address.*
> *I know (that) they're coming.*
> *I'll let you know what happened.*
> *I don't know which book to buy.*

Do you know of a good dentist?
Does he know about the accident?

You *know about* a subject if you have studied it: *She knows about computers.* You *know* a place, a person, etc., if you are familiar with it or them: *He knows Paris quite well.* (For **He wasn't knowing it,* see **simple or continuous?**)

knowledge see **countable and uncountable nouns**

known see **famous**

label see **tickets(1)**

lady see **woman**

landscape see **scenery**

large see **big**

last

1. | TYPICAL MISTAKE: *She was dressed in the last fashion.* |

Last can mean 'final' or 'previous'. So the *last* fashion is the previous fashion – the one before now. The most recent fashion – the one still in vogue – is the *latest* fashion. Compare:

She was dressed in the latest (= newest) *fashion.*
December is the last (= final) *month of the year.*

2. | TYPICAL MISTAKE: *It happened last morning.* |

Last can mean 'most recent'. You can say that something happened *last night/ Sunday/year*, and probably *last evening*, but you must say that it happened *yesterday*, or *yesterday morning/afternoon*. (Compare **near(3).**)

3. | TYPICAL MISTAKE: *It's been cold in the last days.* |

If we say that something happened *in the last week* (or *month*, or *year*) we usually mean 'in the week (etc.) just before this one'. We can say *the last few days* (or *weeks*, or *months*), *the last five minutes* (or *years*, or *centuries*) with the same meaning. But if we say *the last day/days/weeks/months/minutes/years/centuries* (= without *few* or a number) we always mean 'the final one(s) of a period'. Compare:

I haven't seen her in the last week/for the last few days.
She was killed in the last weeks/on the last day of the war.

(For the choice between *take a week* and *last a week*, see **take(3).** For *at last, lastly*, see **end.**)

later see **afterwards**

lavatory see **toilet**

learn

> TYPICAL MISTAKE: *I must learn swimming.*

Learn is not followed by *-ing*. It needs the *to-* infinitive, either alone or with *how, what, when, where, whether, which, who(m)*, or *whose: I must learn (how) to swim/when to plant the seeds.* (See also **hear(2)**.)

leave

1.
> TYPICAL MISTAKES: *He left from Spain. *He left to England.*

When you go away from a place, you just *leave* it: *He left Spain.* Use *leave from* only to explain the starting-point of a journey: *We're flying to Japan tomorrow. We leave (from) London Airport at 10 a.m.*

When you leave one place to go to another, you *leave for* the place you are going to: *He left for England.*

2.
> TYPICAL MISTAKES: *He's left playing football. *When will they be leaving back?*

You *leave* (= go away from) a room, building, job, party, person, or country. *Leave* does not mean 'give up' and is not used with the *-ing* form: *He's given up* (or *left off*) *playing football.* You can ask *When will they be leaving?* but the idea of *back* is expressed by *When will they be leaving for home?*

leaving out words

We often leave out part of a sentence to avoid repetition. The chief problems seem to be:

1. how much to leave out

In these examples, it is correct to leave out the part within the brackets: *He walked slowly, (and he was) wondering where to go; from the 17th (century) to the 19th century.*

2. singular or plural?

When we shorten something with *and* in it, we often have to change from singular to plural. Compare:

chapter one and chapter two
chapters one and two

Notice that if we leave out *the*, the noun becomes plural. We cannot say **the English and Japanese language* unless (which is not true!) they are the same language. We could say *the English(-)and(-)Japanese exhibition*, if it were a single art show, or *the Anglo-Japanese exhibition*.

lecture

> TYPICAL MISTAKE: **She delivered an interesting lesson.*

You *give* or *deliver* a lecture; you *give* a *lesson*, an *address*, or a *talk* (less serious than a lecture). You *make* or *deliver* or *give* a *speech*. All of these are *on* or *about* some subject.

leisure see free(1)

less see fewer

lessen see drop

lethal see fatal

letters

1. sender's address

This is written in the top right-hand corner. Note the order of number–street–town–county–country. The postal town may be written in capitals. The postcode (BrE, = AmE zip code) follows the county, or goes on a separate line. In the British system, the date is in the order day–month–year (but see **dates**). There is now very often no punctuation or indentation, especially in AmE.

---

37 Tunstall Road

BROXBOROUGH

Wilts SN11 9BJ

---

or

```
37 Tunstall Road

BROXBOROUGH

Wilts(hire)

SN11 9BJ

UK

Tel (0439) 336001

3 9 92 or 3/9/92 or 3.9.92.
```

2. business letters

In business letters, the name and address of the firm you are writing to goes on the left-hand side, starting below the line where the date is. It may be indented, but is generally not. If you are continuing a correspondence you may have to quote their reference number.

```
The Manager

Sanvox Radio Co

Bolt Lane

WIGTON

Devon TQ12 2AK

Your Ref: JG PQ17
```

3. the opening (= AmE the salutation)

This is followed by a comma (,) in British use, and in AmE use for a friendly letter, but by a colon (:) for an AmE business letter; not by an exclamation mark (BrE, = AmE exclamation point) (!).

```
Dear Sir(s)/Dear Mrs Bright/Dear Mary,
```

4. some friendly messages

Love is for the family, close friends and people you are in love with. It is not otherwise used between men, or between the sexes, where it might be misunderstood.

My father sends his kind regards/asks to be remembered to you.

Please give my love/regards/best wishes to your mother.

Regards to Bill.

Say hello to Susie for me.

5. the ending (= AmE the complimentary close)

Formal or business letters to strangers that begin *Dear Sir/Madam* end with *faithfully* (esp. BrE)/*truly*. Letters beginning *Dear Mrs Bright* end with *sincerely/best wishes*. The other endings are for letters that begin *Dear Mary. Yours* has a capital Y. There is a comma (,) before the final name, but no full stop (esp. BrE)/period (.) after it.

Yours faithfully/truly (AmE also Very truly yours),
    Peter Simpson

Yours sincerely (AmE also Sincerely yours)/Best wishes,
    Peter Simpson

Yours/All the best/Love,
    Peter

6. typed formal or business letters

These commonly leave a space for the handwritten signature, which is followed by the person's full name and perhaps their position. When a letter is signed by a secretary on someone else's behalf, we use *pp*.

```
                    Mary Greenfield

                  Dr Mary Greenfield
                    Senior Registrar


                     Susan Strike
                  pp Michael Brown
                   Managing Director
```

7. postscripts

These come after the signature and are for afterthoughts. Use PS for the first and PPS for a second, but avoid them in business letters.

```
  PS Betty sends her regards.

  PPS Don't forget to pay the milkman.
```

8. the envelope

The first name comes before the surname. The address starts halfway down, and follows the same order as shown in **1** above. If a man is a *Sir* or a *Rev* (a clergyman) include the first name or initials. The formal style *Esq* (for Esquire) is becoming less common in Britain and is rare in the USA. It is for men only, and is combined with the first name or initials but not with Mr. Any degrees or honours follow it. Your own return address may be put in the upper left-hand corner of the front of the envelope, or on its back.

```
  (Mr) Peter Simpson/(Mrs, Miss, Ms) Mary Greenfield

  Peter Simpson, Esq, CBE

  Sir/Rev Peter Simpson

  Dr Mary Greenfield, FRCP
```

9. addressing business letters

Put *Messrs* (the plural of Mr) before the names of firms that are also people's names. *Co* is for company, *Ltd* for limited, *plc* for public limited company, and *Inc.* for Incorporated (in US English).

> Messrs R J Jones & Co Ltd

Note that in AmE there is a full stop after *Mr./Mrs./Dr.* and sometimes *Rev.*, but the Americans are less likely to abbreviate *Reverend*. (See also **post**.)

lift see ride.

¹like

1a. like/as

> TYPICAL MISTAKE: *She sings as a nightingale.*

Use *like*, not *as*, before a noun or pronoun to mean 'in the same way as' or 'similar to': *She sings like a nightingale.*

1b. like/as

Like can also be used between a linking verb and a noun phrase or verb phrase: *It looks like rain/being another rainy day.*

2. like/as

Use *as*, not *like*, before a noun to mean 'in the position of'. Compare:

> *He plays the viola as a professional* (= he is a professional).
> *He plays the viola like a professional* (= he is not a professional, but he plays as well as they do).

3. like/as/how/the way

Unless a noun or pronoun is involved, *as* is correct, but *like*, *how* and *the way* are all common: *I can dress as/*(informal) *like, how, the way I want.* Notice that *the way* meaning 'the method, the manner' can be used either as a noun or informally to replace *as*. Here it is a noun: *I was surprised at the way* (or *how*, but not **the way how*) *he spoke.* Here, it means 'like this': *Do it this way.* A more formally correct alternative uses *in*: *Do it in this way.*

You will hear people use *like* for *as if*, but do not imitate them. It is not considered to be good English: *?He talks like he's the boss.*

²**like** (verb)

1. ┌───┐
     │ TYPICAL MISTAKE: *I'd like that you sign your name. │
     └───┘

The correct pattern here is: *I'd like you to sign your name.* In 'pseudo-cleft' sentences, *for* is standard: *What I'd like is for you to sign your name.* This *for* is sometimes heard in AmE even in ordinary sentences, especially after *would like*: *I'd like for you to sign your name.*

2. I'd like/I like

Use *I'd like/love/hate* about particular things you want to have or do. Use *I like/love/hate* about your general preferences. Compare:

I'd like a hot drink, please.
I like hot drinks.

(See **asking for things**. For *Would you like . . . ?* see **offers**. For the choice between *like to X* and *like Xing*, see **-ing(1a)**.)

3. like/love/be keen on/be interested in

You *like* people or things that you find pleasant. *Love* is a stronger word than *like*, expressing great affection: *to love your mother; Do you love him enough to marry him?* But to *love* something may just mean to like it very much: *He loves swimming.*
    If you are *keen on* people or activities you find them attractive: *He's keen on football/politics.*
    If you are *interested in* people or things you think they are important, and want to know more about them: *I'm not interested in your problems.* (See **interested.**)

likely

This can be an adjective or an adverb. As an adjective, it may or may not be pre-modified: *The (most) likely candidate is Professor Smith.*
    As an adverb, *likely* is usually pre-modified, usually by *very, quite, more,* or *most*: *They'll very likely arrive late again.* Sometimes the adverb *likely* appears without pre-modification (esp. in AmE), though not at the beginning of a clause: *They'll likely arrive late again.*

linking verbs

Instead of telling you what the subject 'did', like *ate* in *Bill ate a hamburger*, these verbs tell you something about the subject, like *looked* in *Bill looked hungry*. They are followed not by an object but by a 'complement'. This can be an adjective, like *hungry* here; or sometimes a noun phrase, particularly after *be*, like *a nice boy* in *Bill seems (to be) a nice boy.* (See also ¹**like(1b)**.)

1. One set of these verbs tells you the impression that something makes on you.

(a) *seem, appear*: *They seem/*(more formal) *appear happy* (= I think they are happy).
(b) *look, sound, feel, smell, taste*: *The coffee tastes delicious.* (See the examples in **adjective or adverb?**)

2. Another set tells you that the subject becomes (= starts to be) something. The chief verbs here are *become/get/grow/come/go/turn.* Often it does not matter whether you use *be* or the more formal *become,* but prefer *be* for things that happen to you suddenly: *I was/became seasick. I was* (not **became*) *sorry to hear that he'd left.*

    With adjectives, you can often use the informal *get* (see also **get(3)**). The rather literary *grow* means that something changes gradually: *It got/became/grew dark. We got wet/drunk* (not **grew* here).

    Come is used particularly for 'good' changes: *My wish came true.* (But notice *come undone, come unstuck.*)

    Go is used particularly for 'bad' changes: *Everything went wrong.* (Notice that if you *get mad* you become angry, but to *go mad* usually means to become insane.)

    Turn is used particularly for colours: *The leaves are turning brown. Turn* can also signal unexpected changes, often but not always 'bad' ones: *turn nasty; turn traitor* (not **turned a traitor*).

listen see **hear**

little see **big; bit; few**

live see **stay**

long

Long and *for long* both mean the same as *for a long time,* but they are used only in questions and negatives. Compare:

> *Have you been waiting (for) long?*
> *I can't stay (for) long.*
> *She stayed (for) a long time.*

If you use *for a long time* in negative sentences, it may mean something different. Compare:

> *I haven't worked here long* (= I am a new employee).
> *I haven't worked here for a long time* (= it's a long time since I worked here).

(For *a long way,* see **far(1)**.)

longer

1. no longer/more

If things happen *no longer* or *not any longer,* they have stopped happening. You can use *not any more* or (formal) *no more* with the same meaning, but these phrases must come at the end of the sentence. Compare:

> *He no longer* (not **more*) *lives there.*
> *He doesn't live there any longer/more.*

Compare also:

> *The tree doesn't bear any more fruit* (= than the other trees, or than last year).
> *The tree doesn't bear fruit any more/longer.*

2. *Longer* (but not *more*) also means 'for a longer time': *Can't you stay a little (bit/ while) longer?*

look

1. | TYPICAL MISTAKES: **Look to this photo. *I'm looking up for a job.*

When you turn your eyes to see something, you *look at* it: *Look at this photo.* (See also **see(2)**.) When you are trying to find something, you *look for* it: *I'm looking for a job.*

2. look out of/at

When you are inside a room, you can *look out of the window*, or *look out (of the window) at the view*. Someone outside might say *There's a face at the window! He's looking out at the window!*

3. look out for

When you *look out for* someone or something, you try to see or be aware of them or it: *I'll be looking out for you at Paddington Station.*

4. look out

This can be a warning: *Look out! There's a car coming!* (See **warnings**.) In informal BrE, it can also mean 'look for and find': *I'll look (you) out a good book to read on holiday.*

5. look down on/look up to/look to

Look down on means 'feel superior to', and *look up to* means 'respect, revere'. *Look to* means 'look hopefully or expectantly in the direction of': *They looked to automation to solve their economic problems.*

6. look good/good-looking

We say that something or someone *looks good* when we comment on their appearance: *The plan looks good on paper, but will it work? Good-looking* is used only of people, and means 'physically attractive': *a good-looking boy.*

(For more about *look*, see **face**. For *look forward to*, see **-ing(2b)**. For the choice between *to look* and *to have a look*, see **verb or noun?**)

loot see rob

lot

1. *A lot* and *lots* are very common, though rather informal, ways of making comparatives stronger. There are many others: *a lot/lots/some/any/even/still more people; a lot/lots/no/far/rather/*(formal) *considerably less money.*

With plurals, you can also use *a few, (a good or great) many, several* and the numbers: *a few/several/a good many/a great many/five more people.*

With uncountable nouns, and with adjectives and adverbs, you can also use *much, a little, a bit, a good* (or *great*) *deal: a lot/much/a little less money; lots/a bit/a good deal/a great deal better.*

(See **fewer; much.**)

2. a lot/much/plenty

TYPICAL MISTAKES: **plenty money; *too much of noise.*

Before nouns, use *much, more, less, many, several, a little, enough* as adjectives, without *of*, when speaking merely of a number or quantity: *too much noise.*

Use *of* when speaking of proportion. Compare:

Many people (= a large number) *go to Spain in summer.*
Many of those people (= a large proportion) *enjoy the wine there.*

But *plenty, a bit, a lot, lots* and *a good* (or *great*) *deal* always need *of: plenty of/a lot of/lots of money.* (See also **bit; numbers(4).**)

3. a lot/much/many

It is rather formal to use *much, many* in simple statements. In speech, prefer *a lot/ lots*, except in questions and negatives and with *so* and *too*:

'Have you much to do?' 'Yes, I have a lot/a great deal to do.'
(formal) *I have much/great pleasure in declaring this hospital open.*
Thanks very much/(less formal) *a lot.*

But *a lot, lots* are not used with units of time: *Many* (not **Lots of*) *years ago. . . .*

loud/noisy/aloud

Loud is a neutral word, the opposite of *soft: loud music/voices/radio.* Sudden noises are *loud: a loud shout/bang/explosion.*

Noisy is used of unpleasantly loud noises that go on for some time: *noisy children; a noisy office/party/car.*

Aloud and *out loud* mean 'in spoken words': *to read a poem/a letter aloud.*

(For the choice between *loud* and *loudly*, see **adjective or adverb?(6)**.)

love see ²like(3)

low see big

luck

When you *wish someone luck,* you can say:

Best of luck!
Good luck with your driving test.
(more formally) *I am writing to wish you every success in your new position.*

lust see desire

Mac-/Mc-

They both mean 'son of', and it is polite to make sure of the right spelling for any individual name. In Britain (but often not in the USA), *Mc-* is alphabetized as if spelt *Mac-*.

mad

If someone is really insane, we tend today to call them *mentally ill*, or to use such technical words as *schizophrenic*. If they are just silly, we say *Are you mad/crazy/out of your mind?* and complain informally that they are *nutty, batty, barmy* (AmE also *balmy*), (BrE) *bonkers, dotty, bananas* . . . there are many such words.

Informally, *mad (at)* can mean 'angry (with, at)'. If you are *raving mad*, you are very crazy, but if you are *hopping mad* you are very angry. (For *get/go mad*, see **linking verbs(2)**.)

mail see post

make

1. *Make* has some unusual verb patterns. Compare:

He'll make a good husband (= become one).
He'll make her a good husband (= become one for her. This pattern seems to be chiefly used about people).
His mother made him study (= caused him to. Note the passive with *to*: *He was made to study*).
His mother made him a sweater (= made one for him).
His mother made him (into) a criminal (= caused him to become one).
The army will make a man of him! (= cause him to become one).

2. made from/of/out of/with

Made from is especially useful when there is one major constituent that has been transformed, typically by human action: *Flour can be made from wheat.*

Made of is useful when there is one major constituent that has been transformed, but not by human intervention: *Ice is made of frozen water.*

Made out of is useful when there is more than one important constituent, considerably transformed, typically through human action: *Dough can be made out of flour and water.*

Made with is useful when there is more than one constituent but not all of them, and often not the most important, are named: *Dough is made with water.*

3. make it/do it/manage it

When people *make it*, either they cover a distance or they succeed: *Will they make it to the top?*

When things *do it*, they are enough or satisfactory: *I'll add another spoonful – that ought to do it.*

When people *manage it*, they succeed in doing something mentioned before: *Come at six if you can manage it.*

(For the choice between *make* and *do*, see **do.** See also **sort(1); take.**)

man/gentleman/boy/lad/youth/guy/chap/bloke

An adult male is a *man*. *Gentleman* is a polite word used perhaps about a very old man, or when speaking of a man in his presence (*this gentleman would like to see the manager*). *Gentlemen* is used when addressing a male group. You can call a male person a *boy* if he is either a child or much younger than you. *Boys* is used of a man's circle of male friends (*a night out with the boys*) or of soldiers (*our boys out in the East*). *Lad* is a friendly word for a young man or boy. *Youth* means the same thing but is less friendly, being often used about delinquent teenagers. *Guy* is informal. In American use, a mixed male and female group may be addressed as (*you*) *guys*. *Chap* and *bloke* are informal BrE equivalents of *man*. *Man/men*, *lad/lads*, *gentlemen*, *boys*, *guys* and *chaps* can all be used vocatively. *Fellow* also means 'man', and may be becoming old-fashioned, except when *fellows* is used as a plural vocative. (See also **people; youth; woman.**)

manage/run/handle/cope with

When you are in charge of a business or organization, you *manage* or *run* it: *to manage/run a hospital/an office/a shop*. To *manage* or *handle* someone or something also means to make them work properly: *to manage/handle a boat/a class of difficult children*. To *cope with* a problem is to conquer it successfully: *She has to cope with her deafness.*

manager see head

many see lot

mark see stain

marry, marriage

1. | TYPICAL MISTAKES: **Sarah is married with an Indian boy. *His marriage with Sarah surprised his family.*

Use *to* here: *married to an Indian boy; his marriage to Sarah.*

2. | TYPICAL MISTAKE: *Sarah is marrying an Indian boy; they have three children.*

If they have three children, then (probably) they *married*, or *got* (= became) *married*, some time ago: *Sarah married Gopi in 1988. They (got, were) married in 1988. They are happily married/a happily married couple.*

3. marriage/wedding

Marriage is the state of being married: *Theirs has been a very happy marriage.* A *wedding* is the actual ceremony: *They invited us to their wedding.*

masculine, male; feminine, female

Male and *female* refer to a creature's sex, or sexual characteristics: *a male swan/nurse; female frogs/mayors.* (See also **woman**.) When you are asked about your sex on a form, you put M (= male) or F (= female).

Masculine and *feminine* mean 'typical of male/female people'. They also apply to grammar: *her loud masculine* (not **male*) *voice; his rather feminine handwriting*; 'He' and 'she' are masculine and feminine pronouns.

match see game

material see cloth

may/might have

It does not always matter which you use: *I may have/might have met her once, but I've forgotten.* But compare:

> *He may have been drowned* (= perhaps he was drowned).
> *He might have been drowned* (= it was possible, but it did not happen).

(For *May I . . . ?* see **asking for things**. See also **can/could**.)

meet

1. meet/get to know/come across

When you *meet* someone, you happen to go to the same place so that you can start talking if you want to. The word is often used when introducing two strangers: *I'd like you to meet my father.* (See **introductions**.) *Meet* is also used when people arrange to go to the same place: *Let's meet for lunch tomorrow.*

To *get to know* someone is to become familiar with them, through seeing them often: *I met Sue for the first time at Dick's party, but we really got to know each other when we were both working in the shop.*

To *come across* someone is to meet them accidentally: *I met/came across Alan in the supermarket.* In AmE, *meet (up) with* can sometimes also be used like this: *I met (up) with Alan in the supermarket.* (For *meet up*, see **up.**)

2. ⟨ TYPICAL MISTAKE: **I promised to go and meet Maisie in her office.* ⟩

If you meet someone by arrangement, you come together from different directions. The word is not used when one of you is sitting still: *I promised to go and see her in her office.*

3. *Meet with* can mean 'result in' or 'experience the misfortune of': *Their efforts met with success/failure.* It can also mean 'have a meeting with': *President Gorbachev met with Mr Major in London.*

mend see **repair**

menu see **false friends; restaurant(2)**

minor see **elder**

money

The British £20, £10 and £5 notes, etc., are called *twenty-pound note, ten-pound note,* and *five-pound note* (informally *tenner* and *fiver*). In a bank you ask for *twenties, tens* and *fives.* The £1 is now a coin except in Scotland, where £1 coins and £1 notes are both in circulation. The smaller coins are 50p (= pence), 20p, 10p, 5p, 2p and 1p. These are collectively *change. Small change* is the three smallest coins. One-penny coins are called also 1-penny pieces. (See also **cost; pay; spend.**) In the USA, paper money is called *bills* rather than *notes: a $5 bill.* One US *dollar* = 100 *cents.* The most common US coins are 50¢ (a *half-dollar*), 25¢ (a *quarter*), 10¢ (a *dime* – its official name), 5¢ (a *nickel*) and 1¢ (a *penny*). In AmE a *penny* is a coin worth one *cent*, but in BrE a *penny* is a coin worth – one *penny.* In BrE the plural of the coin is *pennies*, but the plural of its value is *pence.* So in Britain one pound = 100 *pence.* In BrE, the amount £2.50 is read out as 'two pounds fifty; in AmE the amount $2.50 is read out as 'two fifty'.

more

You can use *more* to say whether a word is suitable to name something. All the following are correct:

It's more a field than a garden.
I'm no more a painter than you are/than (I am) a poet.
He isn't French any more than I am.

(See also **comparatives.**)

mortal see fatal

most see superlatives

mother see father

much

> TYPICAL MISTAKES: *There weren't much people at the concert. *Much have been said about the greenhouse effect.

Much is used with uncountable nouns, and with a singular verb: *There weren't many people.... Much has been said....* (See **lot.**)

must

1. must/have (got) to/be to

You say *must* about duties imposed by yourself or by a legitimate authority, *have (got) to* and sometimes *be to* about duties imposed or arranged by someone else, whether or not legitimate:

> *I must give up smoking* (= I have resolved to, or at least I accept the need to).
> *I've got to/*(more formal) *I am to give up smoking* (= the doctor says so).
> *He must get up early* (= I say so, or another legitimate authority does).
> *He has to get up early* (= because of his job).

(For the choice between *have to* and *have got to*, see **have(3).**) But note:

(a) This *must* has no past tense, so we use *had (got) to: He had to get up early.* But it need not be transformed by sequence of tense in indirect speech: *'He must get up early.' They said he must get up early.*
    Must is often used about the future; but the future of *have to* is *will have to. Have got to* and *be to* have no future forms, though they can refer to the future:

> *You must water them regularly* (= I advise it).
> *You'll have to water them regularly* (= it will be necessary).

(b) *Mustn't* means that something is forbidden. *Don't have to* and *don't need to* mean that it is unnecessary:

> *You mustn't sit here* (= I forbid it).
> *You don't have to/need to sit here* (= it's not necessary. See **need**).

(c) Note the following contrast:

> *Nobody must know/Nobody is to know* (= there must be complete secrecy).
> *Nobody has to know* (= nobody need know, though some might).

(d) Note also:

> *Must you go?* (= your decision).
> *He says he must go* (= his decision).
> *This problem must be solved* (= my decision).
> *They want/wanted to know whether they must paint it* (= they want/wanted a decision).

2. *Must* is also used about what is likely, or certain. Here, its past and perfect are *must have*:

> *You must be hungry* (= I'm sure you are).
> *You must have been hungry* (= I'm sure you were).
> (esp. AmE) *You have (got) to be joking!*

The usual negative is *can't*, or (esp. AmE) *mustn't*:

> *You can't/mustn't be hungry* (= I'm sure you aren't).
> *You can't/couldn't/mustn't have been hungry* (= I'm sure you weren't).

An alternative is *will*, *won't*. This is rather 'weaker': *You'll be Mr Travers* (= I suppose you are).

3. *Be to* can be used, especially in the past, about something 'foreordained': *Though Abraham Lincoln was born in a humble log cabin, he was to become President of the United States*. (See also **conditionals(2); inversion(6).**)

name

1. name/call

TYPICAL MISTAKE: *His parents named him as Edward.*

Name and *call* both mean 'give a name to'. The verb patterns are:

> *His parents named/called him Edward.*
> *I name this ship the Pequod.*
> *The college is named after/called after/(AmE also) named for its founder.*

Name is used only with actual 'names': *This little wheel is called* (not **named*) *a ratchet.*
Name, but not *call,* can also mean 'say the name of': *Can you name this flower?*

2. name/nominate

They can both mean 'choose, specify'. The patterns here are:

> *They named/nominated him as leader.*
> *He was nominated for the leadership.*
> *They nominated* (AmE also *named*) *him to lead the expedition.*

3. *Name as* can also mean 'identify by name as': *He named them as the traitors.*

nationality

1.   TYPICAL MISTAKE: *French are keen on football.*

With some nationality words, we turn the adjective into a noun and say *the French* (etc.) when we mean all those people collectively: *the French; the Dutch.* With other nationality words, we make a plural noun from the adjective: *the Germans; the Russians.* When all these adjectives are used as uncountable nouns, it means the language: *French/German/Spanish/Japanese is an interesting language.* They all take a capital letter. (See **capital letters.**)

2.   TYPICAL MISTAKE: *a typically Frenchman.*

Some nationality words have a special name for a person from that country: *a Pole; two Swedes; a Frenchman; two Englishwomen.* As they are all nouns, we use adjectives with them, not adverbs: *a typical Frenchman.*

3. When there is a choice, prefer the adjective form for both nationalities and religions: *He's Catholic* (rather than *a Catholic*); *they're Dutch* (rather than *Dutchmen*).

near

1. near/nearby

After a verb, you can use either word: *They live quite near/nearby* (or *near by, close by*). Only *near*, not *nearby*, can be used as a preposition: *a house near here* (*nearby* means 'near here' or 'near there').

Before a noun, you can use *nearby*, *nearer*, or *nearest*, but not (in this sense) *near*: *a nearby tree; the nearest tree* (not **a near tree*). *Near* before a noun is used in certain phrases (*the near future, a near relative*) and can also mean 'almost' (*a near tragedy*) or 'left-hand' (*the near front wheel*) or 'closest to us' (*the near side of the river*).

2. nearest (to)/next (to)

They can both mean 'closest in space; with nothing in between': *the house nearest (to)/next to ours. Next,* but not *nearest,* also means 'directly after now, or after this one': *the next day/chapter; next Sunday; Where shall we go next?*

3. If today is Friday, August 9th, then Sunday, August 11th, is probably *this (coming) Sunday,* and *next Sunday* is Sunday, August 18th. But it is just possible that *next Sunday* can refer to Sunday, August 11th. As for Sunday, August 4th, it is *last Sunday* or possibly *this (past) Sunday*. Both *next Sunday* and *this Sunday* will probably be clear in context; but make sure that you and everyone else knows which Sunday is meant. *The next Sunday* means 'the following Sunday', and can refer to a past Sunday as readily as to a future one. (See also **last(2)**.)

nearly/almost

Often, either word will do: *nearly all the children; almost every time.*

You can say *not/pretty/very nearly. Almost* is not used like that: *You're not nearly old enough. It's very nearly three o'clock.*

You can say *almost any*, and use *almost* before negative words like *never* and *nothing. Nearly* is not used like that: *Almost anyone will tell you.* (See also **never**.)

Use *nearly* about things you might have done, but did not, or that you might not have done, but did: *You nearly ran over that cat!* Use *almost* about beliefs and feelings: *It's almost incredible.*

Practically is used like *almost*, not like *nearly*.

neat see tidy

need

1. *Need* can be an ordinary verb, with an object: *They need help; they don't need help; do they need help?* But when *need* is followed by another verb, there are two patterns, the ordinary verb and the 'modal':

> *He needs to* (= has got to) *study; he doesn't need to study; does he need to study?*
> *He needn't* (= hasn't got to) *study; need he study?*

(If something *need not/does not need to* happen, it is unnecessary. See **must(1b).**)

The modal verb pattern is used only in questions, in the negative, and in sentences with some 'negative' feeling (see **nonassertive**):

> *Nobody need worry.*
> *All you need do is watch it.*
> *One need think only of the health hazards.*
> *I wonder whether I need write to her.*

The things to remember are:

(a) Do not mix the two patterns. You can say *Need we wait?* or *Do we need to wait?* but not **Do we need wait?*
(b) Only the ordinary verb *need* is used after another modal verb: *We may not need to buy one.*
(c) Modal *need* takes the infinitive without *to*; the ordinary verb *need* takes the *to*-infinitive: *You needn't worry/You don't need to worry.* To *be* + -*ed* (the passive *to*-infinitive) can be replaced by the -*ing* form: *The car doesn't need to be washed/washing.*
(d) American English often prefers the ordinary verb, where the British would use the modal. (For the choice between *need* and *want*, see **want(2).**)

2. past and future

You can use either verb pattern about future events:

> *Do you need to/Will you need to/Need you go tomorrow?*
> *You don't need to/won't need to/needn't go tomorrow.*

But in the past, there is a difference of meaning:

> *I needn't have waited* (but I DID wait).
> *I didn't need to wait* (= perhaps I waited, perhaps not).

needless/unnecessary

> TYPICAL MISTAKES: **It is needless to say/***Unnecessary to say that this was absurd.*

The adjectives *needless* and *unnecessary* mean the same thing: *needless* (or *unnecessary*) *risks.* But in addition, the phrase *needless to say* means 'of course', and is used by itself, like an adverb. *Needless* in this phrase cannot be replaced by *unnecessary*, so you must say: *Needless to say, this was absurd*, or *It is unnecessary to say that this was absurd.*

neither/none

1.
> TYPICAL MISTAKES: **Both of them haven't come. *All of them haven't come.*

In negative sentences like this, use *neither* or *not either* about two things, *none* about more than two: *Neither/None of them have come.* (But see **all(2).**)

2. It is considered incorrect to use plural verbs and pronouns after *neither* and *either*, but this is very common in spoken English where *neither* is followed by a plural noun:

> *Neither of the two girls has done her homework.*
> (less formal) *Neither of the two girls have done their homework.*

None can be thought of as meaning 'not one', which is singular, or 'not any', which may be plural. The following are both correct:

> *None of the three men have come.*
> *None of the three men has come.*

But when an extra clause, such as a tag question, is added, only the plural is possible: *None of the three men have come, have they?* (See also **singular or plural?(3).**)

3. neither/either
(a) They are chiefly pronounced /ˈnaɪðə, ˈaɪðə/ in BrE, and /ˈniːðər, ˈiːðər/ in AmE, but both pronunciations are acceptable everywhere.
(b) It is perfectly correct to use *neither* and *either* before more than two alternatives, in sentences like this: *He neither drinks, smokes, nor eats meat.*

4. Where there is a choice, prefer *either, any* with a negative verb, rather than *neither, none* with a positive one: *I don't want either of them/any of them.*

5. The following patterns are available for 'agreeing' with a negative sentence:

> *'I can't afford it.'*
> *'I can't, either.'*
> *'Neither/Nor can I.'*
> (informal) *'Me neither! Nor me!'*

(See also **either; inversion(1); nor.**)

never

You can say *He almost* (or *practically*) *never sleeps*, but you cannot say **nearly never* or **rather never*. (See **nearly.** For *Never have I met . . .*, etc., see **inversion(2).**)

nevertheless/none the less/however/yet/but/(al)though

1. These are all ways of expressing 'contrast'. *Nevertheless, none the less, yet* and *however* often introduce a new sentence which seems surprising after the previous one: *He was exhausted. Nevertheless/However, he went to work as usual.*

Nevertheless, none the less and *yet* can be combined with *and* or *but*: *He refuses to pay, and nevertheless/and yet expects to be admitted.*

2. *Though*, but not *although*, can come at the end of a clause. Notice the word order here:

I hate music lessons; my mum forces me to go, though (more formal *nevertheless, however*).
I hate music lessons, but/(more formal *yet*) *my mum forces me to go.*

Although and *though* can both come at the beginning of a clause; *though* can come in other places too: *(Al)though poor, they seem healthy/They seem healthy, though.*

Clauses introduced by *although, though,* and *even though* cannot stand on their own:

They seem healthy although/though/even though they are poor.
They seem healthy. However, they are poor.

night

1. at night/in the night/by night

There is a difference. For 'when or after it gets dark' say *at night*: *She works here and goes home at night.* Note the contrast between *at nightfall* and *at daybreak*.

For 'at some moment or moments during the night' say *in/during the night*: *He woke up twice in/during the night.* For 'during all or part of the night' say *at night, during the night,* or *by night. At night* contrasts with *during the day*, and is used typically with verbs as an adverbial: *We keep this door locked at night.*

AmE can use *nights* instead of *at night*, typically in short intransitive verb phrases: *She studies days and works nights.*

By night contrasts with *by day*, and is used typically to post-modify noun phrases: *They advertise a tour of Paris by night.*

2. You can say *I've been working all night*, or (less commonly) *all night long, the whole night, all through the night, throughout the night.* But a negative, such as *He hasn't slept all night*, has two possible meanings. (See **all(2).**)

nil see zero

no

1. no/not

> TYPICAL MISTAKES: *There's no much time. *There's not telephone.

No can mean 'not any', and is then used wherever *any* could be used: *no time; no telephone; no shoes; No Smoking!* Where *any* could not be used, the right word is *not*: *not much time; not in winter; not a thing to wear* (= nothing to wear).

2. no/not any

Not any is less formal than *no*, and more usual in speech: *There weren't any/There were no letters.* The same is true about *anybody, anything*: *There doesn't seem to be anybody/There seems to be nobody at home.*

3. S is not C/S is no C

When the complement is a noun phrase, both *no* and *not* are possible in English, but *S is no C* is associated especially with a gradable use of the noun phrase: *She's no fool = She's not a fool.* Otherwise, *S is not C* is favoured: *She's not a fool, but a very perceptive woman. Whales are not fish, but mammals.* Contrast *She's not a teacher* (= she's something else) with *She's no teacher* (= she's not a true, or real, teacher).

4. not/no + comparative (+ than)

Both *not* and *no* are correct here, but *no* + comparative is more emphatic, and is appropriate for surprising news: *The Wimbledon champion is probably not older than 21. Believe it or not, the Wimbledon champion is no older than 15!*

noisy see loud

nominate see name(2)

no more see longer

nonassertive

> TYPICAL MISTAKE: *The door will budge if you push it.

Some words and phrases are typically not used in simple assertive statements. They may accompany negative words like *not, nobody, never*, or adverbs like *only, hardly, seldom*, or certain words with negative force, like *refuse*; or they may be used in questions and the *if-* part of conditional sentences. Grammarians call them 'nonassertive'. One example is *budge* = 'begin to move':

The door will move if you push it.
The door won't move/budge (unless you push it).
The door refuses to budge.

In these sentences, *ever, any, at all, yet* and *either* are nonassertive:

> *We hardly ever meet.*
> *She seldom eats any breakfast.*
> *He hasn't spoken at all.*
> *Can the baby walk yet?*
> *No, and she can't talk either.*

none see **neither**

For *none the less*, see **nevertheless**.

nonsense see **countable and uncountable nouns**

nor

> *George can't drive, and nor/but nor can Mervyn.* This is BrE. If you said *and neither/but neither can Mervyn*, it would be 'world English', and correct everywhere. The British can also say: *'George can't drive.' 'Nor he can!'*

not see **no**

nothing, nought see **zero**

notorious see **famous**

noun before noun

English, like other Germanic languages, often uses nouns adjectivally before other nouns. Instead of *a student of history* we may speak of *a history student*. We can say either *the University of London* or *London University*. Or there may be no choice; we always say *a railway station*, never **a station of the railway*, and (AmE) *a labor union*, not **a union for labor*. Such combinations must be learnt individually. Here are some of the problems:

1. whether to join these compounds with a hyphen, or perhaps to fuse them into a single word. (For some discussion of this difficult question, see **hyphens(1)**.)

2. when to drop the plural *-s* (compare *'s(2)*)

> TYPICAL MISTAKE: **a five-stars hotel.*

If a plural noun comes before another noun we usually drop the *-s* but not always. A book of *cheques* is a *cheque book*, a bar for *snacks* is a *snack bar*. Notice that plural numbers always drop the *-s*: *a five-star hotel*; *a ten-minute walk*.

One or two nouns that end with -s have a special adjectival form when they precede other nouns: a factory that makes *trousers* is a *trouser factory*. But a teacher of *mathematics* is a *mathematics teacher*, and we say either *trades union* or *trade union*.

3. forming a noun–noun combination when you shouldn't

> TYPICAL MISTAKE: *She drank a whole milk bottle.*

A *milk bottle*, a *matchbox* and a *teacup* are containers for milk, matches and tea. Compare:

> She drank a whole bottle of milk.
> You shouldn't keep petrol in a milk bottle.

Be careful of creating combinations that do not exist in English. A *bunch of keys* is not called a *key bunch*, and we say the *manager(ess) of a shop* rather than a *shop manager(ess)*.

4. not forming a noun–noun combination when you should

> TYPICAL MISTAKE: *a company of chemicals.*

This should be a *chemical company*. In the same way, a machine for *sewing* is a *sewing machine*, and a player of chess is a *chess-player*. Look carefully at the examples in your dictionary.

Formations like *chess-player* and *chess-playing* are very common in English, and new ones are constantly being formed. Thus: *record-player; tin-opener* (BrE)/*can-opener* (AmE); *house-painter; child-minder; baby-sitter*. Ambiguity is possible when the first word can be either a noun or an adjective: an *English teacher* can be a teacher of English (noun) or a teacher who is English (adjective). The ambiguity can be resolved in writing by using a hyphen: an *English-teacher* teaches English (noun). In speech the meaning is made clear by where you place the main accent: an *'English-teacher* versus an *English* (adjective) *'teacher*.

5. noun–noun or adjective–noun?

> TYPICAL MISTAKE: *a large departmental store.*

Many nouns have a related adjective. *Departmental* means 'connected with a department', as in *departmental meeting*; but a big shop is a *department store*. In the same way, we speak of *educational standards* and *educational films*, but in connection with people and institutions it is *Education Officer* and *Education Department*; we speak of *seasonal work* but buy a *season ticket*, *postal services* but *post office* and *postage stamps*, and *autumnal colours* but the *autumn term*.

6. It is perfectly correct to leave out the first part of a compound if the context is clear: *I'd like the one in the (shop) window.*

numbers

1. figures or words?

Use figures in mathematics and statistics. Otherwise, most people write small numbers (usually under 10 or under 100) in words, larger numbers in figures. Large numbers are punctuated with commas to mark off the thousands, or in technical writing by spaces: *2,304,791* or *2 304 791*.

Numbers over a million can be written as *6,000,000* or as *6 million*, and millions of pounds or dollars are often written as *£6m, $6m*. (See also **dates**.)

Although £ and $ are written before the number, we say them after it: *six million pounds; thirty-three dollars.*

2. singular or plural?

Plural numbers usually take a plural verb: *90 people have bought tickets*. But if you are giving an opinion about the actual size of the number, use a singular verb: *90 miles is too far to drive*. (See also **fewer/less(2)**.)

3. | TYPICAL MISTAKE: **More 17 people arrived.*

Numbers come before words like *more, less, other, extra, fewer: 17 more people arrived. (See also* **fewer/less(3)**.)

4. | TYPICAL MISTAKES: **They sell eggs by the dozens. *He ordered several hundreds of textbooks.*

You can use *dozens, hundreds, thousands* and *millions* in the plural to refer vaguely to large numbers: *I've told you hundreds (and hundreds) of times*. Otherwise, these words have no plural form:

> *They sell eggs by the dozen.*
> *He ordered several hundred textbooks.*

Numbers are followed by *of* only when they mean 'twelve', 'fifty', etc., out of a group that is identified in some way, rather than just a number: *He ordered several hundred textbooks, including fifty of the new geography series*. (See also **lot(2)**.)

5. When numbers above 100 are expressed in words, *and* is used before any tens or units: *2,503,217 = two million, five hundred and three thousand, two hundred and seventeen*. Some Americans can omit the *and*, especially:

(a) when counting: *one thousand three, one thousand four. . . .*
(b) before numbers from 13 to 99. *Two hundred seventeen* is more likely than *?five hundred three* except in counting.

(c) when the number is used on its own. *Two hundred seventeen* is more likely than *?two hundred seventeen people*.

And cannot be omitted before fractions: *2¾ = two and three quarters*.

Point is used before decimals: *2.75 = two point seven five/two point seventy-five*.

Years are sometimes treated like ordinary numbers, but this is very formal: *(the year) 1688 = (the year) one thousand six hundred and eighty-eight*. Usually, however, years are treated like this: *(the year) 1688 = (the year) sixteen eighty-eight*. A year that ends in 01 to 09 is read out like this: *(the year) 1905 = (the year) nineteen (oh) five*.

6. Numbers above 100 can sometimes be named digit by digit, as in referring to London buses (*the two five three* for *Bus Number 253*) or telephone numbers, which have special conventions. *0171-435-6892* is *oh one seven one–four three five–six eight nine two*. *0* is usually *oh*; *22, 33*, etc., are usually *double two, double three*, etc., in BrE; *222, 333* etc., in BrE are often *treble two, treble three*, etc., or *two double two, three double three*, etc.; *00* is often *hundred* and *000* is often *thousand*, particularly in AmE. So *222-5000* can be *two two two–five oh oh oh*; or in BrE it can be *two double two–five oh double oh* or *treble two–five treble oh*; or, especially in AmE, it can be *two two two–five thousand* or sometimes *two two two–five zero zero zero*. (See also **billion; money; zero.**)

objective see **aim**

occasion see **chance**

occur see **happen**

of

1. | TYPICAL MISTAKE: *a friend of me.*

This needs the 'double genitive'. Instead of *one of my friends*, you say *a friend of mine*. It is used only about things that belong to people: *this daughter of yours*.

   Note that *a photo of Susan's* is one that belongs to her, but *a photo of Susan* shows her as its subject.

2. that was very kind of you

Notice this pattern. It means 'you were kind to do that': *It was sensible of him to refuse.*

3. A surprisingly frequent printing error consists in the replacement of *of* by *or* or *or* by *of*. Such errors can cause great confusion, because sometimes the result ALMOST makes sense – but not quite. Bear this possibility in mind when you are confused by a passage or English. (Did you spot the mistake?)

4. Both *of* and *for* are used in official names, as of these two real organizations: *Institute for Complementary Medicine; Institute of Contemporary Arts*. Make sure you get the preposition right when writing the name – or when looking it up in an alphabetical list. (See also **'s; verbal adjectives; word and preposition.**)

offers

TYPICAL MISTAKE: *Do you like to wash your hands?*

The polite way to say this is: *Would you like to wash your hands?* A waiter might say:

Would you like some more coffee? Another way to say it, less formally polite, is: *Do you want . . . ?*

When offering food or drinks, we often say: *Have a banana! Have some more coffee! How about a banana? Help yourself to coffee.* But not *Eat a banana! *Drink some more coffee!* When offering to buy someone a drink in a pub, you say: *What would you like? What can I get you? What will you have? What are you having?*

When offering to do something, you say: *Can I take a message? Would you like me to take a message?*

older see **elder**

on see **at; with**

one

1. one, ones

> TYPICAL MISTAKE: *This is my car and that's my brother's one.*

The pronoun *one*, plural *ones*, is not used after possessives or after the word *own*: *This is my car* (or *mine*, but not *my one*) *and that's my brother's.*

2. You can say: *Give me this one, that one, the red one(s), the one(s) in the corner.* But do not use *ones* in the plural directly after *these, those, any, many, few,* or the numbers: *'How many do you want?' 'I'd like four, please.'* It is perfectly correct to use *ones* where an adjective comes in between: *I'd like these blue ones.*

3. one day, etc.

> TYPICAL MISTAKES: *I saw her on one evening. *Let's get together once!*

Use *one* with words about time. Do not add *on*: *I saw her one evening.* (See **a and the(3); at(2,3)**.)

One day and *once* can both mean 'at some time in the past': *I saw her one day/once in the supermarket.* But *once* particularly means 'only one time, not twice': *I've only seen her once.* So *Let's get together once!* can only mean 'not twice'. The meaning intended is probably: *Let's get together some time!*

4. every one/everyone

> TYPICAL MISTAKE: *He's eaten everyone of the chocolates!*

Everyone, anyone and *someone* mean 'every, any, some person'. They are not used about things, and are not followed by *of. Every one, any one* and *some one* mean 'every, any, some single thing or person'. Compare:

He's eaten every one of the chocolates.
Everyone passed the exam.

No one is spelt in the same way for either meaning:

No one failed.
No one room is big enough.

5. English has an indefinite personal pronoun with the forms *one, one's, oneself*: *One can't be sure, can one? One must do one's best. One shouldn't blame only oneself.* This *one* is sometimes used with forms of *you*, and (like such pronouns as *everyone* and *someone*) with forms of *they, he,* or *she,* as in this example from *Webster's Dictionary of English Usage*: 'When one is very old ... your legs give in before your head does.' (G.B. Shaw)

The use of *one* with forms of *you* or *they* is not now appropriate in formal writing. The use of *one* with forms of *he* is especially common in AmE, in writing as well as in speech.

The use of *one* with *one, one's,* and *oneself* is standard in spoken and written BrE, and in AmE is fully acceptable and frequent, too. But when *one* is modified by a relative clause, the rules are different. The following sentence is standard in both BrE and AmE: *One who does his best will eventually get what he wants.*

6. oneself

Note the spelling of this pronoun as one word. The rather rare *one's self* is not a pronoun, but a noun phrase: *According to Buddhism, one's self is an illusion.*

only

The problems here are about word order:

1. In speech or informally, *only* typically goes between the subject and the verb, and the intonation makes the meaning clear:

Alan only builds houses here.
Alan is only building houses here.
Alan should only build houses here.

But in writing, *only* should be placed just before the word or words it refers to:

(a) *Only Alan* (= no one else) *builds houses here.*
(b) *Alan only builds* (= he doesn't sell) *houses here.*
(c) *Alan builds only houses* (= nothing else) *here.*
(d) *Alan builds houses only here* (= nowhere else).

Somewhat more formally, *only* can follow such words or phrases:

Alan builds houses here only (= nowhere else).
Alan builds houses only (= nothing else).

But this can cause ambiguity:

> *Alan builds houses only here* (ambiguous between (c) and (d), but typically read as (d)).

The same rules apply to *only* with adverbials of 'time-how-long':

> *Alan only stayed a moment* (informal).
> *Alan stayed only a moment* (neutral).
> *Alan stayed a moment only* (more formal).

But with adverbials of 'time-when', not all these positions are possible. A typical mistake is: **Alan arrived a moment ago only* (or *yesterday only*). This should be: *Alan only arrived a moment ago* (or *only arrived yesterday,* informal), or *Alan arrived only a moment ago* (or *only yesterday,* neutral).

2. not only . . . but (also)

> TYPICAL PROBLEMS: *?She not only looks after the children but the shop, too.*
> *?He doesn't only sell petrol but also repairs cars.*

Not only and *but* must link the same kind of word – two verbs, two nouns, etc.:

> *She looks after not only the children but the shop, too* (two nouns).
> *She not only looks after the children but also teaches them* (two verbs).

The verbs in this pattern are not made negative with *don't, doesn't, didn't*: *He not only sells petrol but also repairs cars.*

3. *Only* can be modified by *virtually,* but not by *almost* or *nearly*: *'Addled' combines virtually only with 'eggs' or 'brains'.* An equivalent is *almost exclusively*: *'Addled' combines almost exclusively with 'eggs' or 'brains'.*

open see **fasten**

opinion

1. | TYPICAL MISTAKE: **According to my opinion, she's wrong.*

Say *In my opinion. . . .* This is rather a formal word for what someone believes. You can say:

> *I am of the opinion that* (= I believe) *she's wrong.*
> *George is of the same opinion* (= he agrees).
> *We had a difference of opinion* (= we disagreed).
> *What is your opinion* (= what do you think) *of this dress?*

(See also **think.**)

2. An *opinion* can be *honest, firm, personal, popular, mistaken, strong,* or *unjustified.* It can also be *high* (= favourable) or *low* (= unfavourable). It cannot really be *true* or *untrue,* since those words apply to the facts that people have the opinions about.

opportunity see chance

other

1. *Other* is not used after *an.* Instead, use *another:*

> *Will you have another biscuit?*
> *I don't like these shoes. May I try some others?*

But you can say *one other* (see **a and the(3)**): *I have one other brother besides Peter.*

2. ┌───┐
│ TYPICAL MISTAKE: **Charles is playing with some other girls.* │
└───┘

This sounds as if Charles is a girl, too. You can say he is *playing with some girls,* or *playing with some other boys.* (See **different(2).**)

3. You can say *One or other answer/of the answers is probably right,* or *One or another answer/of the answers is probably right.* Both *one or other* and *one or another* are correct. The first is favoured in BrE, the second in AmE.

4. some . . . or other

> *I'll do it somehow or other.*
> *Someone or other is sure to know the answer.*

Or other is used to reinforce the indefiniteness of indefinite words beginning with *some.* (For *on the other hand,* see **hand.**)

outside

1. outside (of)

In BrE, write *They live outside the town,* though *outside of the town* is also acceptable in AmE. However, it seems that *outside of* in this sense is now creeping into BrE, too.

2. outside of (= 'apart from, except for')

They've published nothing outside of a few poems. Here, the *of* is obligatory in BrE as well as in AmE – but this use of *outside of* seems more American than British.

3. outside/out

Compare:

> David's outside. Let's eat outside.
> David's out. Let's eat out.

If David is *outside*, he is close to the building that we are in. If we eat *outside*, we do it in the garden. But if David is *out*, he may be miles away working or playing football. If we eat *out*, we go to a restaurant. The opposite is *eat in* (= 'eat at home').

over see above

overlook see face

overrun see conquer

own

1. | TYPICAL MISTAKE: *He has an own car.*

Own is always used with a possessive: *my, your, his, Helen's, Britain's*, etc. (except in the BrE phrase *an own goal*). If you mean that he *owns* (= possesses) a car, say: *He has a car of his own.* You can also say *He has his own car*, but that could also mean that he has HIS car rather than, or in addition to, someone else's.

2. | TYPICAL MISTAKES: *This is a table of her own making. *I bought a picture of Bill's own painting.*

You must say *that she made herself, that Bill painted himself.* The fixed expression *of one's own making* is used of abstract and usually bad things, and cannot be extended to other verbs like *paint*. You could say *It's a problem of her own making.* We also say an action is somebody's *(own) doing*, if they did it: *This must be your doing.* (For *on one's own*, see **alone**.)

pain

TYPICAL MISTAKE: *My back is paining.*

Your back can *ache* or *hurt*, or you can have *a pain* in your back. *Pain* is indeed used as a verb, but in modern English it does not refer to physical pain. It means 'make someone unhappy': *It pains me to hear you say that.* (See also **countable and uncountable nouns**.)

pair

TYPICAL MISTAKES: *Where's the scissor? *I bought two new white trousers.*

Things that come in two parts joined together, like scissors, trousers and spectacles, are thought of as plural: *Where are the scissors?* These words are not used with numbers. You can say *I bought some white trousers*, but the way to show how many things you are talking about is to use *pair* or *pairs*: *I bought two pairs of white trousers.*

pants/trousers/knickers, etc.

1. TYPICAL MISTAKE: *a new white pant.*

All these words are plural: *some new pants; a pair of pants.* (See **pair**.)

2. In BrE, a man's undergarment is called *pants* or *underpants*. The woman's undergarment is called *knickers, pants,* or *panties.* A man's (or a woman's) outer garment is called *trousers. Slacks* is a rather old-fashioned word for casual trousers, and short trousers are *shorts.*

In AmE, *pants* are trousers for men or women; *slacks* (not an old-fashioned word) are casual trousers for men or (chiefly) women; *trousers* are for men only. The man's undergarment is *underpants*; the woman's, *panties. Shorts* are either underpants for men or short trousers for men or women, while *knickers* are knee-length trousers that fasten tightly just below the knee and are worn with long socks. British women wear *tights*; American women wear *panty hose.*

paper see **countable and uncountable nouns**

past/passed

> TYPICAL MISTAKES: *Summer is passed. *He past the exam.

Use *passed* as part of the verb *pass*: *He passed the exam. Summer has passed.* Otherwise, use *past*, which is not part of a verb. *Past* can be a noun: *He forgot the past*; or an adjective: *the past summer*; or a preposition: *He swam past the boat*; or an adverb: *He swam past.*

past perfect

> TYPICAL MISTAKES: *I had gone to Spain last summer. ?She told me what happened.

The past perfect tense (*had gone*, etc.) does not simply mean that something happened a long time ago. It is used when we speak of two past events, to show that one happened before the other. Compare:

> *I went to Spain last summer* (= one past event).
> *She told me what had happened* (= two events; 'it' happened before she told me about it).

patient/customer/client/guest

Doctors, dentists and hospitals have *patients*. People who sell things, in shops or otherwise, have *customers*, though we sometimes speak of the *clients* of a smart dress shop, for instance. People who provide services, such as lawyers, accountants, social workers, many psychotherapists, and hairdressers have *clients*, except in the case of hotels, which have *guests*.

pay

1. > TYPICAL MISTAKE: *How much did you pay the shoes?

You *pay* sums of money. You *pay* people. You *pay* bills, subscriptions, fares, fines, taxes, etc. But when you buy goods or services you *pay for* them: *How much did you pay for the shoes?* (See also **cost**.)

2. pay (up)

> TYPICAL MISTAKE: *He's already paid up the rent.

To *pay up* is to pay money you owe, even though you would rather not. It does not take an object. (See **up**.) Compare:

> *He's already paid the rent.*
> *Come on then, pay up!*

But *paid up* can mean 'paid in full': *My rent is all paid (up) till the end of the month.*

people

1. people/man/mankind, etc.

People is the usual word for our species in general. *Man* is particularly used when contrasting us with animals. *Mankind* is perhaps rather an emotional word: *to work for the good of mankind.* If *man* and *mankind* seem to exclude women, you can say *humans, human beings, humankind,* or *the human race.* We usually say *he* about *man,* *it* about *mankind, humankind, the human race.*

2. *People* in the ordinary sense is a plural noun: *People want their clothes to fit.* If you need a singular word, it is *person.* The plural *persons* is formal or legal: *the police department that deals with missing persons.* (See **person.**)

A *people,* plural *peoples,* means a nation or tribe: *a seafaring people; the peoples of Africa.* This sense can take plural verbs and pronouns. (See **singular or plural?**)

per

This means 'for each' or 'during each'. It is a formal word used about money and measurements. The ordinary word is *a(n)*: *36 miles per gallon; £300 per/a week; The wine costs 60p a/per glass* (but not **They sell it per glass.* This should be *They sell it by the glass*).

person

You can say *He's a sensible man* (or *person*); *she's an interesting woman* (or *person*). But if we do not know someone's sex, or it does not matter, we say *Only one person answered the questions correctly.* Today *person* is often used in such combinations as *spokesperson, chairperson* (for *spokesman, chairman*). The plural of these nouns can be *-persons* or *-people,* though *-persons* is favoured (*chairpersons*) except in the older *salesperson, salespeople.* Avoid using *individual* for *person.* It is correctly used when we contrast one person with the rest of a group: *the rights of the individual in society.* (See **people(2).**)

pick see up(2)

picture, photo, etc.

TYPICAL MISTAKE: **There's a kangaroo on this picture.*

Even though these things are flat, we use *in: in this picture/photo/drawing/poster*, etc. (also *in the mirror*).

piece

This is the general word for a part of any solid substance. A *bit* is a small piece: *a piece* (or *bit*) *of bread/paper/wood/glass*. A *slice* is a flat piece that has been cut off: *a slice of bread/meat/cake/sausage*. A *chunk* or *hunk* is a big thick uneven piece: *a chunk of bread/wood/coal*. A *lump* is big and heavy: *a lump of lead/clay* (but also *sugar*). A *block* is a straight-sided piece: *a block of stone/ice*.

pillow/cushion

Pillows are on beds, and have washable covers called *pillowcases* or *pillow slips*. *Cushions* are on sofas and chairs, and have less washable covers called *cushion covers*. *Pillows* are typically oblong and *cushions* square.

place

1. place/room

> TYPICAL MISTAKES: *Is there place for her in the boat? *I'm afraid there's no place on this shelf.

Place and *room* can both mean free space to be used for a purpose. A *place* (countable) is a single particular area, point, or position. *Room* (uncountable), or *space* itself, is the word you use when you are looking for a large enough piece of unoccupied space. Compare:

> *Is there room for her in the boat?*
> *Yes, that place in the corner is free.*
> *I'm afraid there's no room on this shelf.*

2. > TYPICAL MISTAKE: *There was a terrible fire in the neighbouring place.

A *place* is a position: *We're looking for a good place to camp.* It may be a seat, bed, etc., available to be used: *a place at the table.* It may also be a town, country, island, etc., but the word is used only when the actual name is mentioned or understood. Compare:

> *There was a terrible fire in the neighbouring town.*
> *They live in a place called Kendal.*

3. Very informally, someone's *place* is their house or flat: *We're staying at my aunt's place.*

(For *take place*, see **happen.**)

plate/platter see bowl

play see game

pleasant

Pleasant/nice/good/fine/friendly; beautiful/lovely/charming/delightful/enchanting; marvellous/wonderful/fascinating are all words for praising things, people, or events. *Pleasant* and *nice* are the most general: *a pleasant, nice* (or *good*) *trip; pleasant, nice* (or *fine, good*) *weather; a pleasant, nice* (or *friendly*) *voice, person.* The other words are stronger. *Beautiful* is for women, children, or things (not usually men) that are very good to look at, but we also speak of *beautiful weather* and *beautiful music.*

Lovely is strong and also general: *a lovely girl/party/view/house/meal. Charming, delightful* and (even stronger and used chiefly by women) *enchanting* are for things or people that greatly attract you: *charming manners; a delightful smile; an enchanting child. Marvellous* and *wonderful* are for things so good that you are astonished: *a marvellous restaurant; a wonderful idea. Fascinating* things are very interesting: *a fascinating book/city/theory.*

pleased/satisfied/content(ed)

They all mean 'happy because of what has happened, or because of the way things are'. *Satisfied* means 'completely pleased':

She was rather pleased with my work.
She was never satisfied (= completely pleased) *with my work.*

Content and *contented* mean 'quietly happy, not wanting any change'. There is no difference between them except that *content* is not used before a noun. They apply to emotional happiness, not to critical judgment: *contented cows; He seems quite content(ed) just to sit in the sun all day.* (See also **verbal adjectives.**)

pleasure see countable and uncountable nouns

plunder see rob

positive see sure

possibility see chance

post

You stick *stamps* (= *postage stamps*) on a letter or a *card* (= *postcard*, often a *picture postcard*) before sending it *by post*. (AmE also *by mail*.) The *post office* puts a *postmark* on the stamp. You can send your letter *second class*, or *first class* which is quicker, or *Special Delivery* if you are in a great hurry. Letters from Britain for abroad go either *by air* (= *airmail*), with *Swiftair*, quicker and more expensive, or *by surface mail* (= *by sea*), which is slower and cheaper. You can use an *airletter*, which needs no extra envelope and will go anywhere in the world by airmail.

If you are sending something heavy, you choose whether to send it by *letter post* or by *parcel post*, which have different rates. If you are sending something valuable, you can get a *Certificate of Posting*, or send it *recorded delivery* (= for documents, uninsured) or by *registered post* (= for money, etc., insured).

You *post* (AmE also *mail*) your letter in the *postbox* (AmE *mailbox*) or in the red, pillar-shaped British *pillar box*. Another word is *letter box*, which also means the slot in your door for letters delivered by the *postman* (AmE also *mailman*):

Is there any post (AmE also *mail*) *for me?*
My reply is in the post (AmE also *mail*) *– you'll get it tomorrow.*
They sent the tickets by return of post (= in the next collection, AmE *by return mail*).

You can also buy a *postal order* (AmE *money order*) at a post office. The person in charge there is the *postmaster* or *postmistress*. And you can send a *cable* to a country abroad, though there are now no longer internal *telegrams* in Britain. (See also **letters**.)

practically see nearly

prefer

1. | TYPICAL MISTAKES: **I prefer cats than* (or *from*) *dogs, *I prefer cats the most.*

You *prefer* things *to* other things: *I prefer cats to dogs.* (For *preferable to*, see **elder(2)**.) You may *like* things *best* or *most*, or *better* or *more* than other things, but do not use these words with *prefer*: *I prefer cats. I like cats (the) best/(the) most.*

2. I'd prefer/I'd rather

Use *I prefer* about your general habits, *I'd prefer* about a particular choice now. (See also **²like(2)**.) *I'd rather* is less formal, and has both meanings. Compare:

Where do you prefer to (= *Where would you rather*) *sleep?* (= what are your habits?)
Where would you prefer to (= *Where would you rather*) *sleep?* (= please choose!)

prevent see stop

price see cost

prisoner

Someone who is captured is *taken prisoner*. If they are then not allowed to escape, they are *held* or *kept (a) prisoner*:

> *The guerrillas took her/us prisoner.*
> *They held her (a) prisoner/held us prisoner for three months.*

Captive and *hostage* behave like *prisoner*.

prohibitions

> TYPICAL MISTAKE: **It is not allowed to park here.*

The short way to forbid anything is: *No Parking! No Smoking!* You can also say:

> *Bathing is forbidden.*
> *Photography is prohibited inside the church.*
> *Smoking is not allowed during takeoff.*

pudding/dessert/sweet, etc.

A *pudding* is boiled or baked and eaten hot: *chocolate/apple pudding*. It need not be sweet; *steak-and-kidney pudding* is made with meat, and *black pudding* is a kind of sausage. But the British often say *pudding* (informally *pud*) for any kind of *dessert*. They also call it *sweet* or (informal) *afters*.

put

1. | TYPICAL MISTAKES: **Please open that tap. *I'd better shut the light.*

You *turn on* or *turn off* taps, or anything controlled by a tap: *Please turn on that tap.*
    You *put on, turn on,* or *switch on* anything electrical controlled by a switch or a button, and you *turn* or *switch* (not usually *?put*) it *off: I'd better turn off the light.*
    You *light,* and you *put out,* anything that actually burns: *to put out a candle/a cigarette.* You *turn out* things that give light or heat, controlled by a switch or by a knob to be twisted: *to turn out the light/an oil lamp.*

2. You *put on* and *take off* clothes and makeup. (See also **fasten.** For the choice between *put* and *keep,* see **keep(1).**)

put up see stay

put up with see stand

quarrel/argument/dispute/controversy/row

A *quarrel* is an angry *argument*. (You can have an argument that is quite friendly.) A *dispute* is usually a public quarrel between groups: *industrial disputes*.

A *controversy* is a public argument, and usually takes a long time: *the controversy over the question of global warming*. A *row* is a noisy quarrel, either private or public: *to have a row with one's wife*.

questions

1. Questions are used for many other things besides asking for information. They may express criticism (*What's the idea?*), or be used for making a suggestion (*Have you tried boiling them?*), or for invitations (*Why don't you come round on Sunday?*), or introductions (*Have you two met?*), or offers (*Can I help you?*), or requests (*Could you stop a minute?*), or instructions (*Will you be quiet(?)*).

2. question marks (?)

You need not write a question mark after questions used as requests, exclamations, or greetings: *Would you mind opening the door(?) How do you do(?)*

Do not write a question mark after reported questions: *She asked how I was.*

3. question tags (also called tag questions or tags)

> TYPICAL MISTAKES: *You've been there, isn't it? *It happened in October, or not (or not so)?*

Here, you must use either a question tag or, informally, *(is that) right?*: *You've been there, (is that) right?*

In BrE and AmE, question tags are variable. *Isn't it?* can follow only a sentence that includes *it is*, or a noun that is replaced by *it*. Compare:

You've been there, haven't you?
It's Thursday, isn't it?

We use the same tense and the same grammatical person as in the main sentence. Auxiliary verbs are repeated, ordinary verbs are replaced by *do, does, did,* and nouns are replaced by pronouns:

John can't drive, can he?
John can drive, can't he?

All these sentences can be used either as true questions (= am I right?) with rising intonation, or as a sort of statement (= I think I'm right!) with falling intonation. The difference, of course, does not appear in writing, except that the tags with falling intonation may sometimes be punctuated with . or ! instead of ?

In the examples so far, negative tags follow affirmative sentences and affirmative tags follow negative sentences. But positive tags can follow positive sentences: *So you know the answer, do you?* The effect is often to express scepticism (= I suspect you really don't know the answer).

Negative tags can also follow negative sentences, with the effect of peevish annoyance: *Oh, he can't, can't he?* (This needs falling intonation).

quick(ly) see **adjective or adverb?**

quiet/silent/calm

Quiet things or people make very little noise: *a quiet voice/engine; Be quiet! I'm phoning. Silent* means 'with no noise at all', and particularly 'without speech': *a silent meal/film/prayer. Quiet* is used about private or secret doings: *I'll have a quiet word with her.* You may tell someone to *keep quiet* when you want them to keep a secret: *Please keep quiet about what happened yesterday. Quiet* can also mean 'peaceful; not fussy or active': *a quiet life/village/Christmas.*

Calm is close to that meaning. It is used particularly about water and weather: *a calm lake/evening. Calm* people are not excited or worried. You tell people to *keep* or *stay calm* if they seem frightened or angry.

quite

1. *Quite* has two meanings (stronger and weaker) that may be confused:

(a) = 'completely'. It is used here with words that imply an 'absolute' degree, and that could not be used with *more* or *very*: *quite dead; quite enough; I saw it quite clearly; I don't quite understand; quite the best film; for quite other* (= completely different) *reasons.*

(b) = 'fairly'. This is for gradable adjectives and adverbs, and similar verbs: *He drives quite fast; you can do it quite easily; I quite enjoyed it.*

To avoid confusion between the two meanings, it is sometimes clearer to use *completely, absolutely,* or *entirely* for the first, and *fairly, somewhat,* or *rather* for the second.

2. quite a

When this is used before nouns about quantity, it means 'a considerable': *It took quite a while/quite a time* (or *quite some time*). *He understands quite a lot/quite a bit of German* (not **quite much*).

Quite a is used informally before other nouns, to mean 'a remarkable': *That was quite a party!*

Before adjectives, *quite a* means 'a fairly', as in **1b** above: *quite a long way.*

3. quite/fairly/rather

In BrE, *quite* is the same as *fairly*, and they are both weaker than *rather*:

> *His English is quite/fairly good* (= it is adequate).
> *His English is rather good* (= I am praising it).

But in AmE, *quite good* can mean 'very good'. Note the following minimal pair, with intonation indicated:

> ∨
> *It's quite good* (BrE = 'not very good').

> ∧
> *It's quite good* (AmE = 'very good').

Quite and *fairly* can also mean 'enough', and *rather* can mean 'too much'. Compare:

> *It's quite early* (= early enough).
> *It's rather early* (= too early).

4. not quite

Not quite the is possible: *He's not quite the man he used to be.*

> *Not quite a* is generally to be avoided:

> *?It's not quite a way to the station* (say *It's not a long way, not far* . . .).
> *?There's not quite a difference* (say *There's not much difference*).

In some important respects, *quite* is 'assertive'. (See **nonassertive.**)

rare(ly) see **scarce**

rather see **prefer(2)**

ready see **finish(1)**

reason see **chance**

record/recording

A *record* is a disc (other than a CD) that reproduces sound. When we speak of the performer, we say *a record by Elvis Presley* (as we would say *a book by Agatha Christie*), but *a record of folk music*. A *recording* is a record, a CD, a tape, or a video. We say *a recording of his voice*.

reduce see **drop**

reflexives

The reflexive pronouns are *myself, themselves*, etc. Note the distinction, made here only, between *yourself* (singular) and *yourselves* (plural). Reflexive pronouns are used with verbs whose subject and object are the same thing, or the same person. The problems are about when to use them and when not to. (See also **one(6)**.)

1. | TYPICAL MISTAKES: **Comb yourself! *They behaved themselves very badly.* |

Some transitive verbs can be used either reflexively or with another object. You can *enjoy yourself* or *enjoy* the music, *hurt yourself* or *hurt* someone else. Other verbs can be used reflexively, or with another object, or with no object at all. You can *dress* or *dress yourself* (same meaning), or *dress* the baby. The transitive verb *comb* is not like that. You must say: *Comb your hair!*

The verb *behave* (opposite *misbehave*) is used in two ways. If you *behave* in a particular way, you act in that way. We do not then use the reflexive pronoun: *They behaved very badly.* If you simply *behave*, or *behave yourself*, you act properly: *I hope the children will behave (themselves) at the wedding.*

2. | TYPICAL MISTAKES: **Shut the door behind yourself! *I said to me.... *We sometimes visit us.*

The reflexive pronouns, not the ordinary personal pronouns *you*, *me*, etc., are used after prepositional verbs, such as *look at* and *look after*: *She looked at herself in the mirror.* These pronouns are not otherwise used after prepositions that describe position or direction in space, even when they refer to the subject of the verb: *Shut the door behind you!*

But they ARE used when we speak of a person's inside feelings: *I said to myself....*

The reflexive pronouns cannot mean 'each other': *We sometimes visit each other.*

3. When you buy or make or get something for someone, you say: *I bought my husband a tie* (or *a tie for my husband*). If it is for yourself, you use a reflexive pronoun: *I bought myself a tie.* (Of course, if you leave out *my husband*, *herself*, etc., it is not clear who the tie or the dress is intended for.)

4. | TYPICAL MISTAKE: **'Who made this cake?' 'Myself!'*

Do not use the reflexive pronouns to answer this sort of question. Say: *'I did!'* or *'Me!'*

5. However, reflexive pronouns can be used to reinforce nouns or other personal pronouns: *'Do you believe in ghosts?' 'Oh yes. Of course, I myself have never seen one* (or *I've never seen one myself...)'*.

Reflexive pronouns can even be used instead of other personal pronouns in nonfinite clauses: *He made everyone else nervous while remaining calm himself* (or, more formal, *while himself remaining calm.*)

6. (by) oneself

If you do something *yourself*, you do it personally. (*Do-it-yourself*, or *DIY* for short, means making or repairing things yourself instead of paying a workman to do it.) If you do something *by yourself* you do it alone, or without help. Compare:

> *She went there herself* (= instead of sending someone else).
> *She went there by herself* (= alone).

7. *Themselves* is hard to use as a gender-neutral singular pronoun: *?Someone has hurt themselves.* Alternatives include the awkward *?himself/herself* and *themself*, an admirable pronoun that is, however, not in current usage. (See also **he or she(1c).**)

relative clauses

1. These clauses are like adjectives, and they are of two kinds. One kind tells you which noun we are talking about. These are 'restrictive' or 'defining' relative clauses:

> *This is the woman (whom) I love.*
> *She went to the room where she works.*

The other kind simply tells you more about the noun in question. These are 'nonrestrictive' or 'nondefining' clauses:

> *This is Sandra, whom I love* (= and I love her).
> *She went to her room, where* (= and that is where) *she works.*

The problems are about word order and punctuation:

> TYPICAL MISTAKES: **Edward has a pet goat who writes silly TV scripts. *My husband who writes silly TV scripts wants a divorce.*

The first sentence sounds as though the goat writes the scripts! The second sounds as though I have several husbands. The clause must always follow the noun it refers to. If it can be omitted (= is nondefining), separate it from the rest of the sentence by commas:

> *Edward, who writes* (= and he writes) *silly TV scripts, has a pet goat.*
> *My husband, who writes silly TV scripts, wants a divorce.*

Compare: *A man who writes silly TV scripts has offered Carlo a job.*

2. Relative clauses are different from 'appositional' clauses. Compare:

> *The fact (that/which) we discussed yesterday is important* (= restrictive relative).
> *(The fact) that we discussed it yesterday is important* (= restrictive appositive).

Technically, *that* is a relative pronoun (like German *der/die/das*) in relative clauses but a subordinating conjunction (like German *daß*) in appositional clauses.

remember

1. TYPICAL MISTAKE: **I don't remember to have met him.*

When you take care not to forget something you must do, you *remember to do* it: *'Don't forget to feed the parrot!' 'Yes, I promise I'll remember to feed the parrot.'*
    Afterwards, when you call back into your memory what you did, you *remember doing* it: *'Did you feed the parrot?' 'Certainly I did. I remember feeding it/*(more formal) *having fed it.'* (See **-ing(1b)**, and compare **forget**.)

2. remember/remind

> TYPICAL MISTAKE: *Please remember me to feed the parrot.*

When you make someone else remember something, you *remind* them: *Please remind me to feed the parrot.*

repair/mend/fix/correct

> TYPICAL MISTAKE: *They're correcting the motorway.*

You *repair* anything that is worn or broken: *They're repairing the motorway; to repair shoes/the video.*

Mend suggests the repair, as by sewing, of something torn: *to mend socks/a shirt.* *Mend* or *fix* suggests simple repairs on something broken or faulty: *to mend a broken toy/a hole in the road. Fix* is less formal than *mend*, but in AmE *fix* is the more likely of the two. You *correct* mistakes: *to correct proofs/exam papers.*

All four verbs are used transitively, with either the faulty thing or the fault itself as object: *to correct proofs/to correct mistakes in proofs.*

requests see asking for things

respective/respectively

> TYPICAL MISTAKE: *She sat by her respective telephone.*

Respective means 'belonging to each one mentioned', so it needs a plural noun. Compare:

> *She sat by her (own) telephone.*
> *We sat by our respective telephones* (= she by hers and I by mine).

The corresponding adverb is *respectively.*

> TYPICAL MISTAKE: *Noam Chomsky and Ludwig Wittgenstein lectured on linguistics respectively philosophy.*

This should be: *Noam Chomsky and Ludwig Wittgenstein lectured respectively/ respectively lectured on linguistics and philosophy. They lectured on linguistics and philosophy respectively.*

Note that *respectively* not only separates, but orders. Chomsky is the linguist; Wittgenstein, the philosopher.

restaurant

1. restaurant/café/cafeteria/snack bar/coffee shop/hotel/inn, etc.

These are public eating places. A *restaurant* is more serious and usually more expensive than a *café*, which serves lighter meals and (in Britain) no alcohol. A *cafeteria* is a self-service restaurant. A *snack bar* has small things such as sandwiches. A *coffee shop* is somewhere between a café and a snack bar. A *hotel* has bedrooms as well as food, and a small hotel may be called an *inn*. The eating place in a factory or office is usually called the *canteen*, and in a school or college it is the *refectory* or *dining-hall*. Soldiers eat in the *mess*.

2. At a restaurant, you first find somewhere to sit:

'Is this table free?'
'No, I'm sorry, it's reserved (or taken).'

Then you choose your meal from the list of food, the *menu*, and wait to be served:

'Waiter! Waitress! (or Miss!)'

The waiter or waitress comes to take your order:

'Is there a set lunch?' (this is not called the *menu*).
'I'll have the trout, please.'
'I'm afraid the trout's off' (BrE = 'finished', *There's no more trout*).
'I'd like fish and chips' (it may say *French fries* on the menu).
'Would you like (not **Do you want) salad?'*
'No, I'd rather have peas, please.'
'Anything to drink, sir?'
'What would you like for dessert?'

Afterwards, you ask for the (BrE) *bill*/(AmE) *check*:

'We'd like separate bills/checks (or to pay separately), please.'
'Excuse me, I think there's a mistake!'

You leave a *tip* for the waiter, unless service is included on the *bill/check*.

ride

A *ride* is a journey on an animal, or in or on a vehicle: *a bus ride; a ride on an elephant/a scooter*.

We speak of a free *ride* in someone else's vehicle. If they take you to a place you want to go to, we usually say *lift*. Compare:

I gave the child a ride on my back.
Can you give me a lift to the station?

right(s)

> TYPICAL MISTAKE: **I demand my right.*

A *right* is something to which someone has a morally or legally just claim. In the singular, but not in the plural, it is usually followed by the *to-* infinitive: *the right to strike; mineral rights; I demand my rights!*
(See also **adjective or adverb?(4)**)

road see **street**

rob/steal/loot/plunder/rip off

> TYPICAL MISTAKE: **Someone robbed my camera.*

You *rob* people or places (*of* property), but *steal* property (*from* people or places). Compare:

> *Someone stole my camera.*
> *A gang robbed the bank.*

(You will hear English-speakers using *rob* for *steal*, but it is considered incorrect.)
Loot and *plunder* are used particularly about stealing in violent conditions, such as a war. You loot or plunder either places (like *rob*), or property (like *steal*), but not usually people:·

> *Shops were looted during the riot.*
> *Napoleon looted this treasure from the Vatican.*
> *The army plundered the city, and got drunk on plundered wine.*

The slang phrasal verb *rip off* is used like both *steal* and *rob*:

> *They ripped off my camera* (= they stole it).
> *They ripped me off* (= they robbed me).

In addition, *rip off* can mean 'swindle, cheat': *That used-car salesman really ripped me off!* Property that is looted or plundered is *loot* or *plunder*. The crime of robbing is *robbery*, committed by a *robber*; the crime of stealing is *theft* (or more technically *larceny*, adjective *larcenous*), committed by a *thief* (adjective *thieving*). The slang verb *rip off* has the corresponding noun a *rip-off*, which is more likely to mean a 'swindle' than an actual 'robbery'.

room see **place**

roughly see **about**

route see **way(1)**

's

1. 's or of

> TYPICAL MISTAKE: *The room's window was shut.*

The possessive *'s* is used:

(a) with words for people and animals, but not things. Compare:

> *Mary's flat; the dog's dinner*
> *the window of the room*

(b) with words about time (see **3** below): *a week's holiday; the day's work.* (But do not use *'s* where there is another possessive word. Say *our topic for tonight*, not **our tonight's topic.*)

(c) with certain things or institutions thought of as human. This is particularly true in newspaper writing, where it saves space: *London's traffic; the court's decision.*

(d) in certain fixed idiomatic expressions. These must be learnt: *at arm's length; for heaven's sake; a pound's worth; the ship's doctor.* (See also **sake.**)

Often there is a choice. You can say *It's the duty of a doctor* (or *a doctor's duty*) *to save life.* You can say *the new bank manager's wife* or *the wife of the new bank manager.* But prefer *of* with long, complicated noun phrases:

> *the kidnapping of the child of the man who wrote the pamphlet*
> (certainly not **the man who wrote the pamphlet's child's kidnapping!*).

2. 's or s' or '

After plurals formed with *s*, use *'* alone. The house of the *Johnsons* is *the Johnsons' house.* After irregular plurals, use *'s.* A party for *children* is *a children's party.* After singulars that end in *s*, either *'* or *'s* is possible; in general, the longer the word the more likely *'* alone is: *Keats's poems; Dickens'(s) novels; Euripides' plays.*

> TYPICAL MISTAKE: *The Antrim Mansions Long-Leaseholders Association* (= name of an organization).

This should become *The Antrim Mansions Long-Leaseholders' Association* (= for long-leaseholders) or, rather less appropriately, *?The Antrim Mansions Long-Leaseholder's Association* (= for the long-leaseholder).

By contrast, the following name is written correctly: *the British Residents' Association of Switzerland.*

3. | TYPICAL MISTAKE: **a month holiday.* |

With singular nouns about time, you MUST use *'s: a month's holiday.* With plural nouns about time, you can choose between using the *'s* form and making a compound adjective, which has no *'s: two weeks' holiday; a two-week holiday* (but not **a two weeks holiday*).

4. | TYPICAL MISTAKE: **This house is our's.* |

The possessive pronouns that end with *s* are spelt *ours, theirs,* etc.: *This house is ours.* But write *one's, anyone's, anybody's,* etc.
  Note that *'s* is also short for *is* and *has:*

She's (= she is) *here.*
The train's (= it has) *gone.*

(See also **have(1b); it's(1); who(2).**)

5. | TYPICAL MISTAKE: **This is the friend of Betty.* |

You must say *This is Betty's friend* (= her friend). But it is correct to say *This is a friend of Betty's* (= one of her friends). (See **of(1).**)

sake

The typical patterns with *for . . . sake* are:
  talking for talking's sake; talking for the sake of talking
  (just) for argument's sake (or *for the sake of argument*) *let's suppose she's right.*
But there are idiomatic phrases in which only the first pattern is possible: *art for art's sake; for God's/heaven's/pity's/*(AmE informal) *Pete's sake.* Furthermore, with personal pronouns and single personal names, only this pattern is used: *for my sake* (not *for the sake of me*). But with full names, groups of names and words for people, both patterns are used:

for James Smith's/Mr Smith's sake
for the sake of James Smith/Mr Smith
for the child's sake; for the sake of the child

With words of two or more syllables that end in the sound /s/, ' tends to be used rather than 's. This is true whether or not the phrase is idiomatic, i.e. whether or not both patterns are possible: *for goodness' sake* (idiomatic = 'for heaven's sake'); *for convenience' sake* (= for the sake of convenience).

In most other cases the longer pattern, with *of*, is the one to use: *for the sake of contrast/ornament; ?for contrast's/ornament's sake*

satisfied see pleased

say/tell/speak/talk

These 'speech' verbs are all used in different patterns (see Table on pp. 158–9):

(a) Only *say* can introduce direct speech: *She said* (not **told*) *'I'll be late.'*
(b) *Say* and *tell* usually take an object, which can be a clause. *Speak* (= use words aloud) and *talk* (= have a conversation) usually do not: *I'll speak to her* (not **speak her*) *about it.*
(c) The object of *say* cannot be a person: *He said* (not **said me*) *'Go home.'*
(d) Only *tell* can be used with commands: *She told me* (not **to me*) *to go.*
(e) Only *tell* can have two objects. One of them must be a person: *Tell me a story!*
(f) Although *speak* and *talk* are both 'speech' verbs, they can be contrasted: *'She doesn't* speak *– she talks. She communicates with her fingers in American Sign Language.'* (*Sunday Times* magazine). Here *talk* has been pressed into service to mean 'communicate' and *speak* to mean 'communicate orally'. We suspect that it could have been the other way round: *She doesn't* talk *– she speaks.* Indeed, in other contexts *speak* might be preferred: *Their eyes/gestures/facial expressions spoke.*

scarce/rare

Uncommon and perhaps valuable things are *rare: rare books/flowers*. Ordinary useful things that we have not got enough of are *scarce: Potatoes are getting scarce.*

Rare and *rarely* are used about time: *It was one of my rare visits to Edinburgh. I rarely go to Edinburgh.*

Scarcely means 'only just', or 'almost not': *We've scarcely finished breakfast.*

(See also **hardly; inversion.**)

scenery/landscape/view/scene

Scenery (uncountable) and *landscape* both mean the area of land that one can see. *Scenery* particularly suggests wild beauty to be admired, while a *landscape* may include buildings: *the magnificent scenery of the American national parks; an industrial landscape. Landscape* has spawned several other words with a semi-productive use of *-scape: seascape, cloudscape, moonscape.*

The bit of the scenery that you see from a particular place is a *view: a window with a view of the sea.* If what you see includes people, and things happening, as if on the stage, you may think of it as a *scene: a lively street scene.*

search/seek

> TYPICAL MISTAKE: *I'm searching my brother's address.

If you are trying to find someone or something, you *search for* (or more commonly *look for*, or more formally *seek*) them: *I'm searching for my brother's address.*
    To *search* a place or a person is to look carefully in pockets, clothes, cupboards, etc., for something that may be hidden there: *The police searched him for weapons.*

seashore/seaside see coast

see

1.
> TYPICAL MISTAKE: *I'm not seeing anything.

See in this sense is not used in the *-ing* form: *I can't/don't see anything.* (See **simple or continuous?**)

2. see/look at/watch
If you notice something with your eyes, without meaning to, you *see* it. To direct your eyes at it on purpose is to *look at* it, or sometimes to *see* it, but we cannot tell people to *see* things in the imperative. (If you say *See this?* it is really short for *Do you see this?*) If you pay attention for a while to an event that is happening, or something that may move, you *watch* it. You *see* a photograph but *watch* a film (which you go to *see*). Compare:

> *We saw a dreadful accident on the motorway.*
> *May I look at/see your ticket, please?*
> *They spent the evening watching/looking at television.*
> *Let's watch the boat race!*

(For the choice between *see him come* and *see him coming*, see **simple or continuous?(5)**)

seed see countable and uncountable nouns

seem see linking verbs

seemingly see somehow

senior see elder

series/serial

A *series* is a set of things; particularly stories or books with the same characters or general subject. A *serial* is one long story, printed or told in parts at regular times. So a set of television programmes with a new subject each week is a *series*, but if each programme continues the same story it is a *serial*.

serve

> TYPICAL MISTAKE: *There's lots more stew. Serve yourself.*

The form used in such situations is *Help yourself (to some stew)*. But if you want to *do the honours* by *dishing out* the stew to your guest yourself, the simplest form of words is probably the best. Rather than *Let me help you to some stew* or *Let me serve you some stew*, say just *Let me give you some stew* or *Have some (more) stew*.

settle see **down**

shade/shadow

Shade (uncountable) is any place sheltered from the sun, or the shelter so provided. A *shadow* is the distinct dark shape made when something comes between a light and a surface. You can sit in the *shade* of a tree, or in its *shadow*. But compare:

> *The moon was so bright that it cast (= made) shadows.*
> *The temperature was 35° in the shade.*

shall/will

1. Traditionally, *shall* is used with *I* and *we* to predict the future, and *will* with *he, she, it, you, they*; but this distinction is becoming less common today. *Shall* is rare in AmE statements. Compare:

> *He will (or He'll) miss the train.*
> *We will/shall (or We'll) miss the train.*

It is convenient that the short form *'ll* stands for both *shall* and *will*. The corresponding short-form negatives are *shan't* and *won't*.

2. When we speak of intentions, promises and legal obligations, the position is reversed. *Will* is always used with *I* and *we*, and *shall* is occasionally used with the others:

'Will you take this woman to be your lawful wedded wife?' 'I will' (= in church).
The directors shall publish an annual report (= by law).

3. The Standard English of England always, and American English often, uses *Shall I? Shall we?* for suggestions, offers and requests for advice:

What shall we do? (= advise me!)
Shall we dance? (= a suggestion)
I'll tell them, shall I? (= do you agree?)

4. The Standard English of England may also use *Shall you?* to ask about someone else's intentions. Compare:

Shall you join us? (= is that your intention?)
Will you join us? (= an invitation)

(See also **should; future tense.**)

shampoo see **false friends**

shave

> TYPICAL MISTAKE: **He shaved off his head.*

When you *shave* part of yourself, you cut all the hair from it: *He shaved his head.* When you *shave* something (usually hair) *off*, you cut it off: *He shaved off his beard.*

ship see **boat**

shock see **countable and uncountable nouns**

shoot see **down**

shopping

1. > TYPICAL MISTAKE: **She's gone for shopping.*

You can *go shopping* (see **-ing(3)**): *She's gone shopping.*

2. shop, store, etc.

Store is another word for *shop,* used particularly by Americans. The British call a large shop a *store;* everyone says *department store* if it is divided into sections each selling a different kind of goods. A *chain store* is one of a group of shops in different towns, owned by the same company. A *supermarket* is a large shop where you walk round taking things off the shelves yourself, and pay at the *checkout*. A *hypermarket* is a very large supermarket, with a wider range of goods.

shore/shoreline see **coast**

short

You can say you are a certain amount or number *short*, which means that you have not got enough of something: *When I counted the tickets, I found that I was two tickets short*. But note that *short* means both 'too little' (of amounts, such as money) and 'too few' (of numbers); so you could also say: *I had two tickets too few*. (See also **big**.)

should/would

1. Traditionally, the rule about *should* and *would* is the same as that about *shall* (see **shall(1)**). That is, *should* is used with *I* and *we*, and *would* with *he, she, it, you, they*, as the equivalents in indirect speech, conditionals, etc., of *shall* and *will*:

> *I thought he would* (or *he'd*) *win.*
> *I thought I would/should* (or *I'd*) *win.*

But this distinction is becoming less common today, and *should* in this sense is now rare everywhere. The short form *'d* can be used to avoid the choice between *should* and *would*.

Note that, especially in the English of England, *I should* is often used when giving advice. It is a sort of conditional sentence with the end left out: *I should/I would/I'd take your raincoat (if I were you).*

2. But the commonest use of *should* is with the meaning 'ought to'. Here, *would* is not possible: *Edward should have warned her. I shouldn't have said that.*

3. *Should* is often used for suggestions, offers and requests for advice (compare **shall(3)**):

> *What should we do?* (= advise me!)
> *Should I open the window?* (= an offer)
> *Should David drive you home?* (= do you want him to?)

4. *Should* is also used formally in some conditional sentences: *If you should meet him . . . . Should you meet him . . . .* (See **inversion(6)**).

shut see **fasten**

sick

1. sick/ill

They both mean 'in bad health'. In modern use, *be sick* chiefly means 'vomit', and *feel sick* means 'feel like vomiting': *The cat was sick on the rug. Air travel makes her (feel) sick.*

When the British speak of general bad health, they use *ill* after verbs. *She was/felt/looked ill*, or *He fell/was taken ill*. Americans use both *sick* and *ill* after verbs: *She looked sick/ill*. Both British and Americans use *sick* before nouns (*sick children, sick pay, sick leave*), though Americans can also speak of *ill children*. People who are *ill* (AmE also *sick*) are more often called *the sick* than *the ill*. A British hospital, though not an American one, is likely to report that someone is *critically ill* when they are actually suffering from the result of an accident or a gunshot wound. An American who feels like vomiting is either *sick*, as in BrE, or *sick to his stomach*. However, we all speak of *ill health* rather than **sick health*.

2. *Sick* also has a much wider application than *ill*. People can be *ill* or *sick*; animals are more likely to be *sick* than *ill*; plants can be *sick* only. We speak of *sick societies*, and of the spiritual *sickness* of the soul. *Sickness*, too, is a more general and less technically medical term than *illness*.

3. well/better/healthy

When you are in good health, you *are/feel/look well. Well* is now sometimes used before a noun: *a health check for well women*. When you recover from an illness, you *get well* or *get better. Better* can mean either 'less ill' or 'completely well again'. Compare:

> *He's a little/no/much better.*
> *She's nearly/completely better.*

Healthy means 'physically strong, and not often ill': *healthy children*.

sightseeing

We speak of *sightseeing* and *sightseers* and also, but less often, say *sightsee* (see **-ing(3)**): *We went sightseeing/did some sightseeing; a sightseeing tour; a party of sightseers.* This is the ordinary way to speak of this tourist activity. Less usually, we might say *see the sights*, or a guide might take us round the *sights*.

(Note that we speak of a *visit to* a place, but a sightseeing tour of a city is not a **visit of* it.)

similar see **different**

simple or continuous?

1. the present tense

> TYPICAL MISTAKES: *I learn to play the trumpet. *She isn't usually feeling cold.

Use the present continuous form *am learning* to refer to an unfinished action or process, going on NOW. Use the present simple form *learn* to refer to a permanent action or state. Compare:

> *I'm learning to play the trumpet* (= it is my present occupation).
> *All the children in the school learn to play a musical instrument* (= it is on the school syllabus).

Use the present simple form with *often, usually, sometimes, never*: *She doesn't usually feel cold.*

2. the other tenses

The same sort of difference between simple and continuous exists in the other tenses. In the perfect tenses, the difference is between a 'result' and an unfinished activity or process. Compare:

> *Who's eaten my strawberries?* (= there are none left)
> *Who's been eating my strawberries?* (= some have gone)

In the past tenses, the difference is usually between a definite action or event and a state or process. Compare:

> *They sat down and rested* (= an action).
> *They were sitting down and resting* (= a state).

3. have

> TYPICAL MISTAKE: *She's having flu.

Have is used in the simple form to refer to someone's condition, or to something they possess (see **have**): *She has flu.* The continuous form *be having* is for actions and processes. Compare:

> *John has red hair* (= permanent state).
> *John's having a bath* (= that's what he's doing now).

4. no continuous form

> TYPICAL MISTAKES: *He wasn't knowing that. *Water is consisting of hydrogen and oxygen.

A few verbs can only describe states. These verbs are used only in the simple forms: *He didn't know that. Water consists of hydrogen and oxygen.*

(a) This is usually true of things that happen to us but are not under our control, such as verbs about our senses and feelings:

feel	hear	love	smell
hate	like	see	taste

(and see **6a** below)
But compare:

I see (= understand) *what you mean.*
The doctor is seeing (= interviewing and treating) *a patient.*

(b) Certain verbs about experiences and relations are used only in the simple form. Here are some common ones:

believe	deserve	own	require
belong	know	possess	resemble
consist	matter	prefer	seem
contain	mean	remain	understand

5. see him come/coming

If you *see* someone *do* something, you see the whole process. Compare:

I saw her cross the street (= I saw the whole journey, from one side to the other).
I saw her crossing the street (= I saw her when she was in the middle).

Feel, hear and *watch* can also be used in these two ways.

6. Sometimes it does not matter which form you use. This is particularly true of:

(a) things that happen to our bodies: *My toe hurts/is hurting.*
(b) words for fairly permanent states: *The book lay/was lying on the floor. It's rained/been raining all day.*

since

1. since/for

TYPICAL MISTAKES: *He's been working here since three months. *Have you been waiting since long?*

Use *for* for lengths of time (see **for(2)**). Use *since* for points of time. Compare:

He's been working here for three months/since Christmas.
Have you been waiting (for) long?

2. TYPICAL MISTAKE: *He came to live here since 1984.*

Since never follows a simple past tense. You must say: *He came to live here in 1984;* or *He's been living here since 1984.*

singular or plural?

1. human groups

Words like *family, government, committee, class, team* can take singular verbs if we think of them as a unit, or plurals if we imagine a set of individuals: *The audience was enormous. The audience waved their arms.*

The singular is rather more formal; the plural is often British rather than American: *The class is/are waiting.* However, such nouns are preceded by *there is*, not *there are*: *There was a huge audience for her ideas.*

A singular verb goes with *it, which, that*, and with singular pronouns. A plural verb goes with *they, who, that*, and with plural pronouns: *It's a committee which/that controls local spending.* Human group nouns formed from adjectives are nearly all plural: *the old/the rich/the Dutch/the French* (see **nationality(1)**); *the good are ...* (= people) contrasts with *the good is ...* (= goodness). *The accused* and *the bereaved* can mean one person (singular) or more than one (plural): *The accused must give her name. The accused all plead guilty.*

2. animal groups

Words like *herd, pack, flock* behave like names of human groups: *The herd was/were restless.*

3. anything, etc.

(a) Use a singular verb with the pronouns *anything, everything, nothing, something; anybody, anyone; everybody, everyone; nobody, no one; somebody, someone.*

It is now common even in writing, though considered less formally correct, to use plural rather than singular pronouns after *anybody* and the other 'human' words ending with *-body* and *-one*, especially when these can refer to a mixed group of males and females: *Somebody has left their/(formal) his or her coat behind.* However, singulars are not sexist when referring to males only, to females only, or to things: *Everyone must wear his best trousers/her best skirt.* With tag questions, and certain other added clauses, only plurals are possible when referring to people: *Everybody's here now, aren't they?* (See also **he or she(1c); reflexives(7).**)

(b) *Every, each*: use singular verbs here, except where *each* follows a plural subject: *Every/Each child pays 50p; They each pay 50p.*

As with the pronouns above, these words are now often followed by plural pronouns when referring to people, especially of both sexes: *Every/Each child must bring their/(formal) his or her own lunch.*

(c) *Either, neither*: the plural is less formally correct than the singular: *Is/Are either of them ready?*

In the situation *either ... or, neither ... nor*, the verb should agree with the nearest word. Compare:

Neither my father nor my brothers are coming.
Neither my brothers nor my father is coming.

(d) *All, any, none, some, half*: use either singular or plural verbs, according to whether the word refers to a quantity or a number: *Has any (of the) land been sold? Were any (of the) employees present?*

4. plurals with 'and'

They take a plural verb unless they refer to a single thing. Compare:

> *Bread and butter were both rationed.*
> *Bread and butter* (= bread spread with butter) *was provided at teatime.*

5. their hats, etc.

Things that people each have one of are plural after a plural 'possessor': *They took off their hats. We risked our lives.*

Certain fixed idioms are an exception here: *They took me under their wing* (= protected me).

You can say *From our point of view . . .* if we agree, but *Our points of view differ* if we don't!

6. billiards, etc.

Words for games are singular even if they end with *s*: *Billiards/Draughts/Darts is . . .*

7. number, percentage, proportion

All these words can mean 'some, several'. They then take a plural verb: *There were a number of reasons against it. A large percentage of them are poor. What proportion of students pass?*

8. general nouns

For *politics is/are* (etc.), see **-ics**. For *chapters 1 and 2*, see **leaving out words**. For *90 miles is/are*, etc., see **numbers(2)**. For *there is/are*, etc., see **there**. See also **countable and uncountable nouns; reflexives(7); youth.**

sink see **drown**

sit

Would you like to sit in/on this chair? You *sit in* an armchair or a car or a bath. You *sit on* a hard chair with no arms or a wall or a motorbike.

sleep

> TYPICAL MISTAKE: **We slept early/late last night.*

To *go to bed* (= get into your bed) is different from sleeping. You might say: *We went to bed early/late last night. We couldn't get to sleep* (= succeed in sleeping). The opposite of *go to bed* is *stay up* (= remain out of bed).

To begin sleeping is to *go to sleep* or *fall asleep* (the blend **go asleep* is incorrect), and the opposite is *stay, keep,* or *remain awake.*

slow(ly) see adjective or adverb?(5)

small see big

smudge see stain

snack bar see restaurant(1)

some see any; few

somehow/somewhat/seemingly

Somehow means either 'in some unknown way' or 'for some unknown reason': *She somehow managed to claw her way back to the top. Somehow it doesn't seem important.*

But *somehow* does NOT mean 'to some extent'. That is what the writer of the following passage probably meant, and should have said:

This treatment obviously affects, and somehow (prefer *to some extent) puts a constraint on, the definition of the term 'pragmatics' itself.* (from a conference paper)

The rather formal *somewhat* means 'to some extent'; but the verbs it modifies tend to express duration rather than individual acts: *She was somewhat annoyed. Things have changed somewhat since 1990.*

Seemingly means 'apparently', or 'it seems that'. Compare:

Somehow (= for some reason) *he couldn't get to sleep.*
Seemingly (= it seems) *he couldn't get to sleep.*

some . . . or other see other(4); any

sorry see apologies

sort/kind/type/species/brand/make

1. These are words for groups that share some common characteristic. *Sort* and *kind* are the most general words: *She's the sort of woman you can trust.*

Type is often loosely used in the same way, but strictly speaking it is for things distinguished by some clear-cut difference. The term *species* (plural *species*) is for the classification of plants and animals: *a new type of camera; Charles Darwin wrote 'The Origin of Species'*.

Brand and *make* are for a manufacturer's named class of goods: *a different brand of toothpaste; 'What make of car is it?' 'It's a Renault.'* In BrE the posh word *marque* is sometimes used for prestige cars: *Hispano-Suizas were his favourite marque.*

Note the use of singular *camera* rather than plural *cameras* in *several new types of camera*. In such cases, the singular prevails over the plural in English.

2. *Kind of* and *sort of* can also be used informally to show vagueness or uncertainty in one's classification:

> *They're sort of gardeners-cum-handymen.*
> *He's (a) sort of (a) gardener-cum-general-handyman.*

3. | TYPICAL MISTAKE: **He's a diplomat of kinds.* |

You can say *of sorts* here, an idiom meaning 'of a rather poor quality', but *kinds* is not used in this way.

spare see free(1)

speak see say

specially

1. specially/especially

Strictly speaking, *specially* means 'on purpose', and *especially* means 'more than usually', or 'in particular'. Compare:

> *The hotel is run specially* (= on purpose) *for foreigners.*
> *Their bones are especially* (= more than usually) *fragile.*

But *specially* is often used for *especially*, even by good writers.

2. | TYPICAL MISTAKE: **Especially young people are worried about it.* |

Especially before an adjective means 'more than usually', so this sentence would mean '*people who are more than usually young*'. Instead, write: *Young people, especially* (or *particularly, in particular, above all*), *are worried about it.* (See **word order(1)**.)

spend

TYPICAL MISTAKES: *We spent a year for touring/to tour Europe.*

You *spend* (= use up) money *on* something you pay for, or *on doing* something that costs money: *We spent £500 on repairing the roof.* You also *spend* (= pass) time *in* an occupation, or *doing* it: *We spent a year (in) touring Europe.* Or you *spend* (= waste or sacrifice) time or energy *on* or *in* an occupation, or *doing* it: *Don't spend too long on this job.* (See also **time(1).**)

sport see game

stain/spot/mark/track/smudge

There's an oily stain/spot/mark/smudge on your sleeve. Any of these words might apply to oil. A *stain* is usually caused by a liquid, and is hard to remove. Grass, wine, blood, ink and gravy make *stains.* A *spot* is a small round stain, or a drop of something, and may be easier to remove. A *mark* is any trace left on a surface which would otherwise be clean or plain. Feet leave dirty *marks* on the floor, and car tyres leave *marks* or *tracks* on a muddy road. A *smudge* is a dirty mark made by rubbing. Coal and mud make *smudges.*

stand

1. *Stand, bear, endure,* (BrE informal) *stick, put up with, tolerate* and *abide* can all mean 'experience patiently (something bad)'. *Tolerate* and *abide* are used only about people and behaviour or mental or emotional pain, but the others can be used also about physical pain: *He bore the discomfort as long as he could. I won't tolerate rudeness.* But you could also say: *I can't stand her husband. She has a lot to put up with.*

2. *Stand, bear, endure* and (BrE informal) *stick* are often used negatively with *can't,* and *abide* is used only that way. The patterns are:

I can't stand (or *stick*)	*it*
	seeing it
	*(*to see it)*
	people interrupting
	*(*people to interrupt)*
I can't bear	*it*
	seeing it
	to see it
	people interrupting
	people to interrupt (BrE)

I can't endure	*it*
	seeing it
	to see it
	(*people interrupting)
	(*people to interrupt)
I can't abide	*it*
	seeing it
	(*to see it)
	(*people interrupting)
	(*people to interrupt)

(See also **-ing(1)**.)

3. *Stand for* is used negatively, about behaviour that you will not allow to happen. It expresses indignation, rather like *tolerate: I won't stand for rudeness.*

start see begin

stay/live/stop/put up

> TYPICAL MISTAKE: *They stay in Sheffield.*

You *live* at your permanent home. You *stay* somewhere temporarily. Compare:
> *They live in Sheffield.*
> *They're staying in Sheffield with their aunt.*

To *stop* in this sense is to interrupt a journey, but in BrE it can also mean *stay: We stopped for lunch in Basingstoke. They're stopping* (BrE) *with their aunt.*
> If a friend *puts* you *up*, or (BrE) you *put up* somewhere, you *stay* there: *He offered to put us up for the night.*

steal see rob

stop

1. | TYPICAL MISTAKE: *It never stops to rain.*

When you no longer do something, you *stop doing* it: *It never stops raining.* When you take time for an activity, in the middle of doing something else, you *stop to do* it or *stop and do* it (see **go(1)**). Compare:
> *They stopped listening* (= they didn't listen any more).
> *They stopped to listen/stopped and listened* (= they stopped whatever they were doing, in order to listen).

(See **-ing(1b)**. See also **end(3); stay.**)

2. Note the following pattern:

The interruption stopped me (from) working.

Here, *from* is far more likely in AmE than in BrE. *Prevent* takes the same pattern, but after *prevent*, *from* is likely in BrE as well as prevailing in AmE.

3. If someone grabs your handbag in the street, you shout *Stop thief!*

store see shopping(2)

storey see floor(2)

street

1. street/road

A *street* is between buildings in a town. A *road* usually leads from one town to another. But a town may have grown so big that former roads called *Something Road* or *the Something Road* have become built up and are really streets. (See **a and the(5)**.)

2. in/on the street

BrE favours *in the street/road*; AmE, *on the street/road*: *a shop in Oxford Street* (BrE); *a store on Fifth Avenue* (AmE). However, BrE as well as AmE has *on* in a sentence like *There's ice on the road*; and AmE as well as BrE has *in* in the idiomatic phrase *the man in the street* (= 'the common man, the ordinary person').

3. along the street

If a street or road is flat you go *along* it, but we also use *up* and *down* with the same meaning: *He was driving along/up/down the motorway*. If it slopes, of course, you use *up* or *down* according to the direction.

subject see citizen

subjunctive

Many European languages have a 'subjunctive' form of the verb. In English, it is almost the same as the ordinary 'indicative' form, and usually IS the same as the infinitive. The only differences from the indicative are:

(a) in the third person singular of the present tense: *that she have* (not *has*); *that he bring* (not *brings*).

(b) in the verb *be*, present and past: *if I/he/we/you/they be* (not *am, is, are*): *if I/he were* (not *was*).

The subjunctive is used:

1. In certain phrases such as *God save the Queen! Long live the Health Service! Heaven forbid! Bless you! if need be; as it were; be that as it may.*

2. In 'unreal' conditions, for example *If he were a fly, he could walk on the ceiling.* In formal writing, prefer *if I/he/she/it were* for this sort of sentence. *If I were you* is a very common way of giving advice: *If I were you I'd sell it.* (But see **conditionals(2).**)

3. In certain clauses after *that*, about things that we propose or wish. This subjunctive is commoner in American English. The British may prefer to use *should* here, or just the indicative:

> *I suggest that he (should) close/(or he closes) the shop.*
> *The doctor advised that she (should) go home/(or she went home).*

4. Note the position of *not* in *They recommended that I not leave.* It comes before the verb *leave*, as if *not leave* were a negative infinitive. There is an older English subjunctive negated differently, and the older and newer patterns can be seen together in the following example: *If she be not a witch, I demand that she not be punished.*

5. In many situations where other languages use their subjunctive, English uses its indicative, or sometimes a modal auxiliary, or another construction: *When she arrives, I'll be in the sitting-room. Although she is/may be right, it's too late to change now. I want her to come back.* (See **verb patterns.**)

subway see **tube**

such

1.
> TYPICAL ODDITY: *?I wish I had such a car/such wine.*

The use of *such* to mean 'like that/this, of that/this kind' is too formal for ordinary speech. Prefer: *I wish I had a car like that.* However, it is normal for *such* to mean 'so great': *Don't make such a noise!*

2. *Such as* is a rather formal way to introduce examples: *Wines such as/Such wines as* (or *Wines like*) *Bordeaux are expensive.* (See **[1]like(1).**)

suggest

1. | TYPICAL MISTAKE: *He suggests to ask her.*

Suggest cannot be followed by a *to-* infinitive. The patterns are:

> *He suggests asking her* (see **-ing(1)**).
> *He suggests that Helen (should) ask her.*
> *He suggests that Helen asks her* (see **subjunctive(3)**).

2. | TYPICAL MISTAKES: *Please suggest me what to wear. *I suggested her to go home.*

Instead, say: *Please advise me what to wear*, or *Please suggest what I should wear. I advised her to go home*, or *I suggested (to her) that she (should) go home*, or *I suggested (to her) that she went home.*

sun/sunlight, etc.

Besides being the star round which our planet revolves, *sun* can mean 'light and heat from the sun': *We sat in the sun* (opposite *shade*, see **shade**). *You need sun and fresh air. Sunlight* is chiefly light, but *sunshine* suggests both light and heat: *This plant needs direct sunlight. We sat in the warm sunshine.*

superior see elder

superlatives

1. Regular adjectives and adverbs form their superlatives either with *(the) -est* or with *(the) most*. (For this choice, see **comparatives(1).**) With both these and the irregular ones, you can either include *the* or leave it out: *The lake is (the) deepest at this point. Which car do you like (the) best?*

2. But note that *most* before adjectives and adverbs can also mean 'very'. This *most* is rather formal, and is used only with words that express personal feelings and opinions – and that are also long enough to form their superlatives with *(the) most*. Compare:

> *a very/most beautiful girl*
> *a very* (not **most*) *fat girl*

sure/certain/positive

1. They can all mean 'having no doubt': *I'm pretty, fairly, almost, quite, absolutely* *sure/certain/positive I'm right* (not **rather* or **very*). *I'm not sure/certain how she feels/ where to go* (not *positive*, in negative sentences).

2. surely/certainly

Surely expresses strong belief but at the same time invites confirmation, whereas *certainly* expresses actual knowledge. Compare:

> *Surely he paid?* (= I think he did. He paid, didn't he? He must have paid.)
> *He certainly paid!* (= I saw him do it.)

surprise see **countable and uncountable nouns**

Table: **say/tell/speak/talk**

	(a) Direct speech?	(b) Takes an object?	(c) Takes a 'personal' object?
say	Yes: *She said 'I'll be late.' He said 'Go home.' Don't forget to say thank you. 'I'll be late,' she said.*	Usually. But note: *Let's meet, say, on Thursday. You don't say!* (See phrases)	No
tell	No	Usually. But note: *I promise not to tell!* (= speak your secret) (See phrases)	Yes: *Don't tell Mary! Tell me about* (not **from*) *it.*
speak	No	Not usually: *I'll speak to her about it. Who's speaking?* (= on phone) Object is usually a language: *He speaks* (= is able to use) *German.* (See phrases)	No
talk	No	Not usually: *Can the baby talk yet? I've been talking to/with our neighbour.* Object is usually a language: *They were talking* (= using) *German.* (See phrases)	Yes, when it means 'persuade': *He talked her into/out of going.*

sweet see **pudding**

swim

1. This can mean 'cover a distance, or cross a piece of water, by swimming': *to swim 100 metres; to swim the Channel.*

2. You *swim*, or (BrE) *bathe*, in a *swimming pool*. (The British also say *swimming bath/ baths*, particularly for an indoor one.) Women wear a *swimsuit, bathing suit* (old-fashioned), or (BrE) *(swimming/bathing) costume.* A very skimpy two-piece one is also called a *bikini.* Men wear *(swimming) trunks.*

(d) Used in commands?	(e) Takes two objects?	(f) Takes a clause?	Phrases
No	No	Yes: *She said she'd be late. You must say where you bought it.*	*to say a prayer/a poem/a few words/something/ nothing; He says so*
Yes: *She told me to go. Tell Mary not to worry.*	Yes. One of them must be a person: *Tell me a story! He told me where to go. Tell* (not **say to*) *her you're thirsty.*	Yes. When it means 'find out' it takes a *wh-* clause: *How do you tell which button to press? I couldn't tell what she was thinking.*	*to tell a lie/the truth/ jokes/secrets/a story/the time; I told you so! To tell the truth* (= frankly) *I forgot!*
No	No	No	*to speak one's mind* (= say what one thinks); *to speak the truth* (not **a lie*); *to speak volumes* (= communicate a lot – but typically not orally: *'Their looks spoke volumes.'*)
No	No	No	*to talk* (= express in words) *sense/nonsense; to talk* (= discuss) *business/shop/politics;* (informal) *We're talking serious money here/10 years to life (in prison) here.*

tags/tag questions see questions

take

1.

> TYPICAL MISTAKES: *I'll go and take your file from the office. *You must take your mother's permission.

Do not use *take* for 'fetch, get, obtain': *I'll go and fetch/get/*(BrE informal) *look out your file from the office. You must get/obtain your mother's permission.*

2. *Take* often means 'accept'. You can *take* someone's advice, or *take* the blame for something. It is also used, like *do*, about certain actions; you *take* or *do* tests and examinations, academic subjects and courses of study. But *take* is used in many expressions about which there is no rule (compare the list of words with *do* and *make*, at **do(1)**):

take

action	part in something
advantage of somebody/something	a photograph
care	pity on somebody
a chance	place (see **happen**)
charge of somebody/something	pleasure in something
a decision (= esp. BrE; or *make*. The	(a) pride in something
process is called *decision-making*)	responsibility
exercise	revenge
an interest in somebody/something	a risk
medicine	somebody's temperature
notes (or *make*)	trouble
an oath	turns
offence (= be offended)	a vow (or *make*)

(For the choice between *look, walk*, etc., and *take a look, walk*, etc., see **verb or noun?** See also **bring; place.**)

3. take/last

Both words can be used about time. If an action or process *takes* a certain length of time, you need that time to do it in. If something *lasts* or *lasts for* a certain length of time, it continues to happen or exist for that time. Compare:

> *The repairs took a week.*
> *The fine weather lasted a week.*

Sometimes we can use either word with very little difference. But compare:

> *How long does the trip take?* (= we are in a hurry for it to end).
> *How long does the trip last?* (= we want it to be as long as possible!).

talk see say

tall see big

target see aim

tear/break

> TYPICAL MISTAKE: **This string won't tear.*

Cloth and paper *tear*. String and rope, as well as wood, glass, china, etc., *break*: *This string won't break.* Human bones *break*, but muscles and ligaments can *tear*. (For the choice between *tear* and *tear up*, see **up(1)**.)

technology/engineering, etc.

Technology is applied science, and a *technologist* is someone qualified in it. These are very general words, since they include the application of science to farming, industry, etc. *Information technology*, for instance, is the processing of information by computer systems. *Technology* is now sometimes treated as countable, especially for discussing different types: *the new technologies that are being developed.*

A *technician*, as distinct from a technologist, is a skilled practical worker with scientific equipment, perhaps in a laboratory. This word is also used, for instance, of someone who comes to mend the TV.

Engineering as a university subject is part of technology. You can study *electrical, mechanical, mining*, or *civil* engineering (the last one is concerned with roads, bridges, dams, and so on). People qualified in these subjects are *engineers*, but the word is vaguer and less prestigious than its equivalents in Spanish, French and German. We speak, for instance, of *telephone engineers*, who install and repair the equipment. The British trades union of industrial machine workers is the *Engineers' Union*. In American use, a railway engine driver is an *engineer*, or, on the subway (= underground), a *motorman*.

tedious see dull

telephone

1. I want to say something to Mary Green: I decide to *telephone her/phone her/call her/*(chiefly BrE) *ring her* (NOT **ring to her*). I may have to use a public telephone in a *phone box/call box*, or, (inside a building) *telephone booth*. All these are BrE for what AmE calls a *phone booth*.

I look up her *phone number* in the *phone book/telephone directory*. I find it. I don't have to ask the *operator*. I *dial* her number. I dial 77100. (See also **numbers(6)**.) If Mary is already *on the phone* talking to someone else, her number is *engaged* (BrE)/*busy* (still chiefly AmE, but coming into BrE. AmE also has *Her line is busy*). If not, the phone *rings*. Good! I've got *through (to her)*. Someone picks up the *receiver* and *answers* the phone.

> 'Hello! Could I speak to Mary Green, please?'
> 'Who's speaking, please?' (NOT **talking*).
> 'This is Jason Ross.'
> 'Mary! There's a call for you.' (NOT **a telephone*).
> 'Hold on, please. Just a moment, please.'
> 'I'm afraid she's out. But you can reach her on 52814.'
> 'Hello! Is that 52814?' (AmE also *Is this 52814?*)
> 'No, this is 58214.'

Oh dear. I got a *wrong number*. I decide to call again later. Or I'll ask her to *call me back*. *'Thank you for calling.'*

2. You can *make a local call*, a *long-distance call*, or an *international/overseas call*; long-distance calls used to be called *trunk calls* in BrE. To make a long-distance call you must dial the *STD* (Subscriber Trunk Dialling) code (BrE), or the *area code* (AmE), then the local number. If you don't know the number or the code, ring *Directory Enquiries* (BrE)/*Information* (AmE). You will be charged for the calls you make unless you dial the operator and ask to *transfer the charges* on a call to someone (BrE), or to *call* someone *collect/call collect* to someone (AmE). In both BrE and AmE you can also *reverse the charges* on a call to someone or, less commonly, make a *reversed-charge call*. If you want to speak to one person in particular, tell the operator you'd like to make a *personal call* to them (BrE) or a *person-to-person call* to them (AmE); in AmE you can also ask to *call them person-to-person*.

television/video, etc.

The machine is a *television* (AmE prefers *television set*), a *TV*, or (BrE informal) a *telly*: *I bought a new portable TV*. The people who *watch* or *look at* the programmes are *viewers*. (See also **series/serial**.)

How many TV *channels* (= different wavelengths or stations) are there in your country? Do they have *cable TV*? *pay TV*? *satellite TV*? Do they have *commercials/advertisements/*(informal) *ads*? We saw the Prime Minister *on television* (see **a and the(5)**).

A *video* is either the machine (*video recorder*) that plays and records video tapes, or else one of the recorded tapes: *to watch an exciting video; a film on video.* The plural of *video* (noun) is *videos*; the principal parts of the verb are *videos, videoing, videoed.*

tell see **say**

terrible see **awful**

textile see **cloth**

than see **as**

thank you

1. | TYPICAL MISTAKE: *'Have a drink?' *'Thank you. I'm driving.'* |

Thank you means that you accept an offer. To refuse, say *No, thank you.* Compare:
> *'Have a drink?' 'No, thank you.* (Not **No please.*) *I'm driving.'*
> *'Have a drink?' 'Thank you.* (or *Yes, please.* (esp. BrE)/ = (AmE). *Yes, thank you,* or *Yes, thanks.*) *I'd like a whisky.'*

2. *Thanks* is rather less formal than *thank you.* You say *thank you* (or *thanks*) for things: *Thank you/Thanks for a lovely evening.* (See also **answers.**)

thankful/grateful

| TYPICAL MISTAKE: **We were very thankful for your assistance.* |

When you have warm feelings towards somebody who has helped you, you say: *We were very grateful for your assistance.* You can be *grateful to* people: *We were most grateful to Susan for driving the van.*
   Thankful is used when you are glad that something has happened or been avoided: *I was thankful to get out of the room.*

that

1. that or nothing at all?

Except in formal writing, *that* can be left out in many kinds of subordinate clause:
(a) when *that* is the object, not the subject, of a relative clause. Compare:
> *The house (that) we bought is damp.*
> *The house that faces the river is damp.*

(For the choice here between *that* and *which*, see **which; who.**)
(b) where the surrounding words are simple ones; particularly simple verbs such as *say, think, believe,* or common adjectives such as *glad* or *frightened.* It is a matter of formality. Compare:

> *She says (that) she hates algebra.*
> *She asserts that she hates algebra.*
> *I'm glad (that) he came.*
> *I'm grateful that he came.*

(See also **relative clauses(2).**)

2. that/this/it

All these words can refer 'backwards' to something previously mentioned, or understood from the context; so sometimes it does not matter which you use:

> *'My name's Prjevalski.' 'Could you please spell it/that?'*
> *We bought a tent. It/That/This seemed a good idea.*

But (a) *That* and *this* refer more precisely than *it*. Compare:

> *Read this/that!* (= the paper in my hand).
> *Read it!* (= the book I have mentioned).

That is the usual word for commenting on something that someone else has said: *'I've got a new bike!' 'That's great!'*
This, but not *that,* can refer 'forwards' to something you are going to say: *This is what I want you to do . . . .*
(b) When we refer to the things or people around us, *that* (plural *those*) is the usual word for the ones farther away, and *this* (plural *these*) for the nearer ones: *that man here; this picture here* (note that *that there man* and *this here picture* are nonstandard).
(c) As pronouns, *that, this, it* can be used with the verb *be* about people. Otherwise, these pronouns can refer only to things. Compare:

> *This is my sister. That's Bill. Who is it?*
> *Look at that* (= an insect)*! Can you see it?*
> *Look at that boy! Can you see him?*

(See also **it.**)

the see **a and the**

there

1. | TYPICAL MISTAKE: *'How can you say we haven't any lunch? *The sausages are there.'*

There are two *there*s in English. One is an adverb meaning 'in that place', just as *here* means 'in this place'. The other is the 'existential' *there* used at the beginning of the first sentence above (*There are . . .*). It is unstressed; it comes before the verb, or immediately after it in a question; and it tells us that something exists. Compare:

> *The sausages are there* (= on the table).
> *There* (stressed = on the table) *are the sausages.*
> *There* (unstressed = they exist) *are the sausages.*

2. When you have a choice, prefer the pattern with *there*. It is very common in English: *There's somebody knocking* (rather than *Somebody is knocking*). The unstressed existential *there* is particularly used with *be*, and with other verbs about 'existing' or 'appearing':

> *There seemed to be no one at home.*
> *There remained only one problem.*
> *There appears to have been a mistake.*

There can be left out in certain 'inverted' patterns. (See **inversion(3)**): *Lying on the mat (there) were some letters.*

3. there is/are

Correctly, we use *there is* (or *was*) with singular or uncountable nouns, and *there are* (or *were*) with plurals: *There was a table. There were three chairs. There wasn't enough water.*

But (a) It is perfectly acceptable to begin with *there is* if a singular noun comes first. Compare:

> *There was a table* (= singular) *and three chairs.*
> *There were three chairs* (= plural) *and a table.*

(b) Use *there is* about a single amount. (See **numbers (2)**): *There's £5 to pay. There's only 50 km to go.*

(c) In any case, *there is* is very common in less formal sentences, even before plurals: *There's two cinemas in the town.*

4. there is/it is

Use *there* when something or somebody not mentioned before exists or happens. Use *it* to refer back to something or somebody mentioned earlier. Compare:

> *'Is there anyone downstairs?' 'Yes, there's a boy waiting.'*
> *'Who's that boy waiting downstairs?' 'It's Alec.'*

think

1. think/believe

Both these words can be used about opinions: *I think/believe it's going to rain.* The negative usually goes with *think* or *believe*, not with the next verb: *I don't think/believe they're coming.*

(a) *Think*, not *believe*, is the usual word for statements and questions about people's ideas. *Believe* could not be used here: *How old do you think he is?*

(b) *Believe*, not *think*, is used about the truth (or otherwise) of surprising statements; or about the honesty of the person who makes them. *Think* could not be used here: *She believes everything he tells her.* (For *believe in*, see **believe**.)

2. | TYPICAL MISTAKE: *We're thinking to sell the flat.*

If you *think of* or *think about* doing something, you consider it as a possible plan: *We're thinking of/about selling the flat.*

this see **that**

though see **nevertheless**

through/to/till/until

All these words can mean 'up to the time mentioned'. *Till* is the same as *until*, but less formal. But note:

1. If a shop is closed *from Monday to*/(BrE) *through to/till/until Wednesday*, is it open on Wednesday or not? The Americans say *(from) Monday through Wednesday*, which makes it quite clear that the shop will still be closed on Wednesday. Unfortunately the British do not yet use *through* like that; and *from Monday to Wednesday* is still ambiguous in AmE as well.

2. | TYPICAL MISTAKES: *We'll stay here until the hot weather lasts. *He had reached home till the storm began.*

Till and *until* do not mean 'while', 'as long as', or 'by the time that'. Say *We'll stay here while the hot weather lasts*, or *till the hot weather ends*.
    These words do not mean 'before' or 'when'. Say *He had reached home before/when/by the time the storm began.*

3. When *till* and *until* are used with negatives, they mean that something did not happen before that time, but that it did happen then. Be careful! If we say *The parcel did not arrive till the 17th*, we mean that it DID arrive on that date. If it was still not there on the 17th, we say that it *still hadn't arrived by the 17th.*

4. to/till

| TYPICAL MISTAKES: *We walked till the shops. *Let's stay here to Thursday.*

Till and *until* are chiefly used about 'time', and *to* about 'place': *We walked to the shops; Let's stay here till Thursday.* But there are exceptions!

(a) *Till* and *until* can mean 'up to the place mentioned' if you think of the place as an 'event' in time: *Stay on the train till (it gets to) Sheffield*.
(b) *To* is used about time when we speak of the clock (*it's 5 to 7*; AmE also *5 of 7*) and when an arrangement is moved to an earlier (not a later) time. Compare:

> *We've brought the date of the conference forward to the 17th.*
> *They put the wedding off until the spring.*

(c) Either *to* or *till/until* can be used with *from* (*from Monday to/till Wednesday*) or when we speak of the length of time before something happens (*it's an hour to/till lunch*).

tickets

1. ticket/label

> TYPICAL MISTAKE: *The ticket came off my suitcase.*

A *ticket* is what you buy to pay the *fare* for a journey, or to get into a theatre, a museum, etc. The word is also used for price cards in shops. A piece of paper fastened to an object and giving information about it is a *label*: *The label came off my suitcase. You must read the label on the bottle.*

2. You buy a ticket at the *ticket office* (railway) or (BrE) *booking office* (railway or theatre) or *box office*, or at a *travel agency, travel agent*. On a bus or long-distance *coach* (BrE) you buy your ticket from the *conductor*, or perhaps from the bus driver: *Single to Glasgow, please* (BrE); *One-way to Chicago, please* (AmE). *Two day-returns . . .* (BrE); *two one-day round-trip tickets . . .* (AmE). *Three halves* (= half-price tickets for children) *. . . First-class return/round trip. . . .* (There are two classes on British Rail, though not on buses or the underground. *Second class* is now called *standard class*.)
    Railway tickets are checked by the *ticket collector* at the *barrier* (BrE)/*gate* to the *platform* (BrE)/*track* (AmE) whence the train departs or, on the train, by the ticket-collector or the *guard* (BrE)/*conductor* (AmE). At an airport, you take your ticket to the *check-in desk* of the airline by which you are travelling, where you obtain a *boarding pass*. (Air tickets often come in three classes: *tourist* or *economy*; *business* or *club* class; and *first*.) (See also **transport; travel.**)

tidy/neat/clean

Tidy and *neat* mean almost the same thing. Perhaps *tidy* suggests orderly arrangement (*a tidy desk*) and *neat* implies careful attention to detail (*neat handwriting*). Things can certainly be *tidy*, and perhaps *neat*, without being *clean*.

till see **through**

time

1. spend/pass/waste (etc.) time

To *spend* or *pass* a period of time is simply to use it, either well or badly (see **spend**): *They spent/passed most of their life in Oxford*. If you do something to *pass the time*, or to *kill time*, you do it because you have too much time to fill: *They played cards on the boat, to pass the time*.

To *occupy* somebody, their time, or their mind, is to keep them busy doing something; perhaps because there is too much time: *This game will occupy the children after tea*.

To *waste* time is to use it badly, either on purpose or by accident: *We wasted an hour looking for the shop*.

To *lose*, or *gain*, time is to waste, or get, a useful length of time: *He ran all the way, to make up for lost time. 'I agree,' said Bill, to gain time* (= to give himself time to think).

2. in time/on time

> TYPICAL MISTAKES: *Your beard will grow again on time.* *The train arrived exactly in time.*

In time means either 'eventually' or 'early enough':

> *Your beard will grow again in time* (= eventually).
> *I was just in time to catch the train* (= early enough).

On time means 'at the right moment; neither early nor late': *The train arrived exactly on time.* (See also **at/in/on(2,3)**.)

3. *Time* can mean the length of a period. Here are some useful phrases for that:

> *It's (been) a long time since we met.*
> *I haven't seen her for (quite) some time.* (See also **quite(2)**.)
> *We'll be there in (next to) no time* (or *in no time at all*, or *(at) any moment (now)*).

We use *It's time . . .* when we mean that something ought to happen now. The patterns are: *It's time to go home/time for lunch/time you went* (or *were going*) *to bed/time for me to leave.*

4.
> TYPICAL MISTAKE: *Last time he was employed in the post office.*

Last time does not mean 'in the past'. It means 'on the most recent occasion before this'. Compare:

> *He was formerly/previously employed in the post office.*
> *Last time I saw him he'd got a new job.*

5. | TYPICAL MISTAKE: *The Anglo-Saxons lived here in early time.* |

A *time* can be a period in history. The word is then used with an adjective, or with some sort of supporting phrase. Unless it is used with a 'possessive' (= *of*, *'s*, or a pronoun) it is plural. Compare:

> *They lived here in ancient times.*
> *The town grew up in Queen Victoria's time.*
> *The castle was built at the time of the Norman Conquest.*

times

This is used for multiplication, above the number 2: *Her car cost three times* (or *twice*) *as much as mine.* (For *times* in arithmetic, as in *3 times 12*, see **in/into(2)**. See also **time(5)**.)

timetelling

1. Note these ways of asking or saying what time it is:

> *'What's the time, Sarah?' 'Nearly six o'clock.'*
> *'What time is it by your watch?' 'Just after six.'*
> *'My watch says five past.'*
> *'Excuse me, can you tell me/have you got/do you have the time?'* (= to a stranger).

2.

	02:00	2. 2 o'clock. Two. Two (o'clock) in the morning. 2 a.m.
	14:00	Two (o'clock) in the afternoon. 2 p.m.
	12:00	12. 12 o'clock. Twelve (o'clock) in the morning. 12 a.m. Midday. Noon.
	24:00	Twelve (o'clock) at night. Midnight.
	08:30	Half-past 8. Eight-thirty. Half-past/(not *half after 8). Half 8 (BrE. This does NOT mean 7:30, as it would in German!)

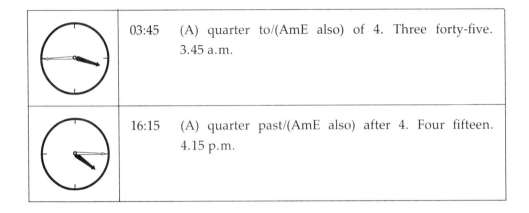

| | 03:45 | (A) quarter to/(AmE also) of 4. Three forty-five. 3.45 a.m. |
| | 16:15 | (A) quarter past/(AmE also) after 4. Four fifteen. 4.15 p.m. |

3. TYPICAL MISTAKE: *It's 4 to 6.*

You can say *5 to 6* (AmE also *5 of 6*) or *5 minutes to 6, 25 past 6* (AmE also *25 after 6*) or *25 minutes past 6*, etc. But with any division of time smaller than 5, you must add *minute(s)*: *It's 4 minutes to 6* (AmE is less likely to use *of* after *minutes*). *It's one minute past 6* (AmE also *one minute after 6*).

4. TYPICAL MISTAKES: *It's 6 o'clock p.m.* *It's 5 past 9 o'clock.*

Use *o'clock* only when speaking of an exact hour. Do not combine it with any other 'time' word: *It's 6 o'clock* (or *6 p.m.*); *It's 5 past 9* (AmE also *5 after 9*).

5. A clock or watch that says 4.55 at 5 o'clock is (*five minutes*) *slow*. If it says 5.05, it is (*five minutes*) *fast*. If it keeps getting faster, it *gains*. If it keeps getting slower, it *loses*.

6. Note that the punctuation *5.30* is British; *5:30* is American. Digital clocks and watches use the American style.

tiresome see dull

to

1. to/for

TYPICAL MISTAKES: *They sent her for buying bread.* *I went to China for learning Chinese.*

Use *to* with the infinitive here: *They sent her to buy bread. I went to China to learn Chinese.*

We do use the pattern *for + -ing* about 'purpose', but it explains the purpose of a 'thing', not a 'person'. Compare:

> *These shears are for cutting grass (with)* (= that is their purpose).
> *I need some shears to cut the grass (with)* (= that is my purpose).

(For the choice between *to* and *for* with 'destinations', see **for(3)**. See also **through**.)

2. to or nothing at all?

> TYPICAL MISTAKES: *You must make her to understand. *Please let me to go!*

In this pattern the infinitive without *to* is used:

(a) after *have, make, let*, and often *help*:

> *You must make her understand.*
> *Please let me go!*

(b) after *see, feel, hear, watch*. (For the choice between *see him come* and *see him coming*, see **simple or continuous?(5).**)

In the passive, however, we use *to* after all these verbs except *let*; *have* has no such passive: *She was made to understand. He was seen to leave.*

toast see **countable and uncountable nouns**

toilet, etc.

This is now the most general word, both for the fixture and for the room. *Lavatory* is chiefly British. *Loo* is a popular informal British word. *W.C.* is not much used.

If you are shy, you can say *I'd like to wash my hands*, or (American) *to wash up*; but this is not always safe, because you might be directed to a room with only a *washbasin* (BrE)/*sink* (AmE)! An American can ask for the *bathroom* or *washroom*, either in a house or in a public place. (American bathrooms almost always do contain a toilet.)

A *public convenience* (BrE) is one in the street. In a theatre, restaurant, or large shop the words are the *cloakroom*, the *gents'*, or the *ladies'*; and (all the following are AmE) the *restroom*, the *men's room*, or the *ladies' room*. The general term is *public toilet* (BrE also *public lavatory*). The term *comfort station* is used in AmE for a public toilet that can be entered from outside a public building. But Americans who want to use one are more likely to ask for the (public) *toilet*, the *washroom*, etc.

After using the toilet, you *flush* it.

tolerate see **stand**

too/very

TYPICAL MISTAKE: *He's too rich now.*

Too with adjectives and adverbs usually means 'more than enough for something; beyond what is good'. *Very* just gives emphasis. So we generally combine *too* with something else in the sentence or context. Compare:

He's very rich now.
He's too rich to bother about that.

But note:

(a) *Only too* can be used like *very*, about good things as well as bad ones. *All too* can also be used like *very*, but only about bad things: *I remember it only/all too well* (= bad. I wish I didn't). *I'm only too pleased to help* (= good. Of course I'll help).
(b) *Not too* is used informally for *not very*: *He wasn't too/*(formal *was none too*) *pleased when I told him* (= he was annoyed).
(For *too tired*, etc., see **verbal adjectives**; for *too* meaning 'as well', see **also; either**.)

tour see journey

town see city

track see stain

transport

1. TYPICAL MISTAKE: *We went home with the bus.*

You must say *We went home by bus*. That is the usual way to speak of a means of transport: *to go by taxi/boat/ferry/hovercraft/helicopter/underground; to travel by sea/by air*. (But *on foot*. See also **journey; ride**.) You can also say *in a taxi, on the ferry*, and so on: *by/on the four o'clock train*. (See **a and the(5)**.)

2. *Aeroplane* is a British word, *airplane* is American, but most people now say *plane*. An *aircraft* (plural *aircraft*) is any vehicle that can fly. *Bicycle* and *motorcycle* are more formal words than *bike* or (esp. BrE) *motorbike*. *Coach* is a British word for a long-distance bus. (See also **tube**.)

3. If I go by bus, I might say: *Where's the stop for the number 12 bus? Where does it go from?* If I *miss* a bus or train, I'll have to *catch* (or *get, take, go on*) the next one.
If I go by train, I say:

When's the next train to Dover? Which platform (BrE)/*track* (AmE)?

Is there a restaurant car (esp. BrE)/*a dining car*/(or, for sandwiches, etc.) *a buffet car; a smoking/nonsmoking compartment; a sleeper*/(AmE also) *Pullman car? Do I have to change?*

If the train is late, I may miss my *connection*.
When I fly, I say:

When's the next plane/flight to Sydney?
Do we go via/by way of Hong Kong?
Can I break my journey there?
What time do I have to check in?

(See also **tickets(2)**.)

travel

> TYPICAL MISTAKE: *our travel to Germany.*

When people *travel*, they go on a *journey, trip, tour*, etc. (see **journey**): *our trip to Germany*. *Travel* as a noun is either uncountable (*air travel, foreign travel*) or plural: *She wrote a book about her travels.*

travel agency, etc.

A travel agency, travel agent, or *travel bureau* books tickets and hotels for you, and arranges package holidays. A *tourist office*, or place labelled *Tourist Information*, will tell you things such as what time the museum opens. Departments that tell you what you want to know, in a railway station or other organization, are labelled *Information* or (BrE) *Enquiries*. You might ask for the (BrE) *enquiry office*.

treatment see countable and uncountable nouns

trip see journey

troublesome see dull

trousers see pants

try

Try and do it means *try to do it*. For more about this, see **go(1).**

trying see dull

tube/underground/metro/subway

These are all words for a railway system wholly or mainly under a city. In London we speak of a *tube* train or an *Underground* station, and travel *by tube* or *by Underground*. The same thing in many other cities such as Paris is called the *Metro*. In some big American cities, such as New York, the word is *subway*; but note that in BrE *subway* means a passage where you can walk under a street. The AmE for this is a *(pedestrian) underpass*.

turn see **linking words(2)**

turn on/off see **put(1)**

type see **sort**

U, V

under/underneath/beneath/below

Under and *underneath* express the idea of 'vertically down from something', and are then the opposite of *over*: *There's a cat under/underneath the bed.* These words can also mean 'covered, protected'. *Underneath* emphasizes this idea: *She wore a green dress under/underneath her coat.* They can mean 'from side to side of something': *He crawled under/underneath the wire.*

Beneath means the same things, but is rather more formal or literary: *The ship sank beneath the waves.*

When we mean 'lower down than something', we usually use *below* (opposite *above*): *Her skirt reaches (to) just below the knee.* Note the phrase *below sea level.* (See also **above**.)

undergo/receive/go through/take

Sometimes you can use more than one of these words: *He underwent* (or *received*) *criticism/injuries/treatment in hospital.*

When things happen to you, particularly difficult or unpleasant things, you *undergo* them. *Receive* is used of things done to you or given to you. *Go through* particularly means that you reach the end of a period of time, particularly a bad one. *Take* can imply that you willingly accept something unpleasant. Notice that you *take* an academic *examination* but *undergo* (or just *have*) a medical one. You *take* a *course* of study or a *course* of action, but *undergo* (or just *have*) a *course* (or *series*) of injections. (See **take(2)**.)

underground see **tube**

unnecessary see **needless**

until see **through**

up

Some verbs can be combined with *up* without changing their meaning: *The hotel is full (up); it's fully booked (up). Let's meet*/(esp AmE) *meet up again soon.*

But with other verbs, to add *up* is to change the meaning:

1. | TYPICAL MISTAKES: *She wants to be a lawyer when she grows. *I tore up my dress on the wire.

Up often means 'completely': *Drink (up) your coffee! Finish (up) the potatoes!* To *tear* something is to damage it by tearing. To *tear* it *up* is to tear it completely, into little bits: *I tore my dress on the wire. He angrily tore up the letter* (not *tear off* or *tear away*).

To *grow* is to get bigger. To *grow up* is to become completely grown, an adult; *grown-up* is an informal word for 'adult': *Growing children need milk. She wants to be a lawyer when she grows up.*

2. | TYPICAL MISTAKES: *I blew some balloons. *She was picking up apples from the tree.

You *blow* your nose, a whistle, a bubble. You must add *up* if you mean 'put air into it': *He blew his horn. I blew up some balloons.*

To *pick* flowers or fruit is to pull them away from their stalks. To *pick* things *up* is to lift them from the ground: *She was picking apples from the tree/picking up apples from the ground.*

(See also **down; keep(2); pay(2)**. For *do up, button up*, see **fasten.**)

upset see **angry**

used to

1. | TYPICAL MISTAKE: *They use to live in Scotland now.

Used to has no present tense. You must say *They live* (or *are living*) *in Scotland now.*

2. | TYPICAL MISTAKE: *I'm used to sit on the floor.

This is a mixture of two patterns:

> *I'm used to* (= accustomed to, in the habit of) *sitting on the floor.*
> *I used to sit* (= I formerly sat) *on the floor.*

In the first, *to* is an ordinary preposition, and can be followed by a noun: *I'm used to Indian food.* In the second, *to* introduces the infinitive. See **-ing(2b)**.

3. | TYPICAL MISTAKE: *Last week we used to go skiing every day.

Used to with the infinitive applies to something that always, or regularly, happened or was true in the past, but (a) is not true now, (b) was quite a long time ago. Compare:

> *Last week we went skiing every day* (= recent past).
> *When we were children we used to go/went skiing every day* (= a long time ago, and we are no longer children).

4. The negatives of *used to* are *used not to/usedn't to* (old-fashioned BrE) and *didn't use(d) to*; the interrogatives are *used he to?* (old-fashioned BrE) and *did he use(d) to?*

usual(ly)

> TYPICAL MISTAKE: **It's raining, as usually.*

The phrase is *as usual*. It means 'as is common; as usually happens'. It is short for *as is usual: It's raining, as usual* (or *as always, as ever*).

vacant see free

verb or noun?

Many words for physical actions are used both as a verb and as a noun. You can *look* at something, or *have/take a look* at it. There is little or no difference of meaning. Perhaps the choice of noun rather than verb means that the action is more deliberate, and has a definite beginning and end.

1. With some of these nouns, but not all, you can use *take*, particularly in AmE. They all go with *have: to rest = to have/take a rest*. Sometimes *have* turns a verb into a rather informal noun: *to think, try, read = to have a think, a try, a read* (esp. in BrE).

2. With nouns about 'movement', you can often use *go for*, too: *to walk, stroll = to have/take/go for a walk, a stroll*.

3. Transitive verbs can form a noun with *give: to wash, clean, sweep, wipe, dust something = to give it a wash, a clean, a sweep, a wipe, a dust*.

verb patterns

This is a complicated subject, about which a good dictionary will help you. Here are some of the patterns that most commonly 'go wrong':

1. verb + object

These are the 'transitive' verbs.

(a)

> TYPICAL MISTAKES: *We went into a café to refresh. *You'll really have to exert.

You must say *refresh yourselves, exert yourself.* You can also *refresh your memory, exert influence,* and so on, but there must be an object of some sort. Use your dictionary if you are not sure about the transitivity of a verb. (See also **reflexives.**)

(b)

> TYPICAL MISTAKES: *Did you enjoy during your holiday? *We were discussing about politics.

This common mistake is to put an unnecessary preposition, here *during* and *about,* between a transitive verb and its object. (The object of *enjoy,* of course, can be a reflexive pronoun.) You must say: *Did you enjoy your holiday? Did you enjoy yourself? We were discussing politics.*

Here are some more verbs about which people make this mistake:

answer   *Please answer the question* (not *to* it).
describe   *They described their journey* (not *about* it).
mention   *He mentioned your new book* (not *about* it).
obey   *He obeyed his mother* (not *to* her).
regret   *She regretted her decision* (not *for* it).
resemble   *She resembles her sister* (not *to* her).
study   *He's studying history* (not *about* it).

(c)

> TYPICAL MISTAKES: *I must rectify that this is without foundation. *He reassured that things were improving.

Unlike some verbs (*emphasize, insist*) with the same sort of meaning, these verbs cannot take a *that-* clause as sole object. You must say: *I must rectify this false impression/insist that this is without foundation. He reassured us that things were improving* (you *reassure* people, not facts).

2. verb + adjunct

> TYPICAL MISTAKE: *It was hard work, but she plodded.

Intransitive verbs like *plod* are not used alone. They need what is technically called an 'adjunct'; that is, an adverb, or a prepositional phrase. (Do not confuse them with verbs that need an adjective or a noun. See **linking verbs.**) You must say: *It was hard work, but she plodded on/away.*

3. verb + *to-* infinitive

> TYPICAL MISTAKE: *He accepted to go.*

You can *agree to go* or *refuse to go,* but *accept* is not used in this way. You must say: *He agreed to go* (or *accepted the invitation*). (See also **help; know; learn; suggest.**)

4. verb + object + adjunct

These transitive verbs need an adjunct (adverb or prepositional phrase) as well as just the object.

(a)

> TYPICAL MISTAKES: *Please put the rice. * They've chopped the tree.*

You must say: *Please put the rice in the pot/on the stove* (etc). *They've chopped the tree down/into firewood* (etc.).

Here are some more verbs, or senses of verbs, like that:

chase *She chased the children away/out of the room* (etc. Not, in this sense, just *She chased them.*)
clip *Clip the brooch on/to my coat* (etc. Not just *Clip it.*)
hang *Hang your coat up/on the hook* (etc. Not just *Hang it.*)
lug *She lugged the trunk upstairs/into the house* (etc. Not just *She lugged it.*)
shoo *I shooed the dog away/out of my garden* (etc. Not just *I shooed it.*)
suck *The current sucked him down/under the water* (etc. Not just *It sucked him.*)
throw *I threw the letter away/into the fire* (etc. Not just *I threw it.*)

(b)

> TYPICAL MISTAKE: *I sprinkled the water.*

You *sprinkle* water *on* something, or you *sprinkle* something *with* water: *I sprinkled water on the path; I sprinkled the path with water.* Some more verbs like that are *scatter, smear, splash, spray, spread.*

(c)

> TYPICAL MISTAKES: *He swept the dust. *I'll rub some polish.*

You can *clean, dust, rub, sweep, wash,* or *wipe* a thing or a place to make it clean, but you cannot use these verbs in this way about the dirt or the polish itself. You then need the pattern verb + object + adjunct: *He swept the room. He swept the dust away.*

(d) Using the wrong object.

> TYPICAL MISTAKE: *We must familiarize this principle to the students.*

This sentence uses the right pattern, but the wrong way round. The object should be a person, not a fact. You should say: *We must familiarize the students with this principle.* (See also **inform.**)

5. verb + object + *to-* infinitive

(a) Using the pattern when you should not.

> TYPICAL MISTAKES: *They prevented me to come.* *He beguiled her to buy it.* *This necessitated us to borrow more money.*

You can *allow, forbid, permit,* or *persuade* somebody *to do* something, but *prevent* and *beguile* are not used in this way. You must say: *They prevented me from coming* (see also **stop(2)**). *He beguiled her into buying it.*

You can *oblige* or *force* somebody *to do* something, but *necessitate* is an ordinary transitive verb: *This necessitated another loan* (or *further borrowing*).

(b) Not using the pattern when you should.

> TYPICAL MISTAKES: *They permitted to her to stay.* *He was forbidden from going.* *They petitioned the government that it should release him.*

You must say: *They permitted* (or *allowed*) *her to stay. He was forbidden to go; they forbade him to go. They petitioned the government to release him* (or *for his release*). (See also **expect; find(3); ²like; make(1); to(2); want(1).**)

6. verb + two objects

These are 'ditransitive' verbs like *give* and *buy,* which can be followed by two nouns: *Give the child an apple. Ask him a question.* The pattern is verb + indirect object + direct object. Without changing the meaning, you can say: *Give an apple to the child. Ask a question of him* (formal).

(a)

> TYPICAL MISTAKE: *Show to Alan your photos.*

If you put the indirect object first, do not include the preposition unless the indirect object is long or contrasted with another: *Show Alan your photos,* or *Show your photos to Alan.*

(b)

> TYPICAL MISTAKES: *She proved us her efficiency.* *Remind him his appointment.* *He shared me his lunch.*

These verbs will not accept the ditransitive pattern. They can be used either in the simple verb + object pattern, or with a following preposition. Compare **4(c)** above:

She proved her efficiency (to us). Remind him (of his appointment). We shared his lunch, or *He shared his lunch with me.* (See also **explain; make(1)**.)

verbal adjectives

The *-ed* participle of many verbs is used as an adjective. From the verb *delight* we make the form *delighted*, and can say *I'm absolutely delighted*, or *the delighted children*. There are two problems here:

1. They are not true passives of the verb from which they are formed. An ordinary passive can go with the preposition *by*: *A tiger* (= one particular one) *frightened Tim = Tim was frightened by a tiger*. But we say *Tim is frightened* (= afraid) *of tigers* (= all tigers). As with other adjectives, the difficulty is to choose the right word or pattern to follow these verbal adjectives. Here are some common ones:

absorbed	*a. in a book*
accustomed	*a. to the climate* (see **-ing(2b)**)
alarmed	*a. at the news; a. to hear it*
amazed	*a. at you/it; a. to hear it; a. that he came*
amused	*a. at it; a. to hear it; a. that she did it*
annoyed	*a. with you; a. at it; a. to hear it; a. that he failed*
ashamed	*a. of you/it; a. to tell you; a. that he failed* (This is really an adjective.)
astonished	*a. at you/it; a. to hear it; a. that he came*
composed	*c. of it/them* (see **comprise**)
connected	*c. with it*
contented	*c. with it; c. to stay here*
convinced	*c. of the truth; c. that it's true*
delighted	*d. at the prospect/with his present; d. to meet you; d. that he came*
disappointed	*d. in/with you; d. at/about it; d. to hear it; d. that he failed*
disgusted	*d. with you; d. at it*
disinclined	*d. to go*
dressed	*d. in red*
engaged	*e. in/on a project*
engrossed	*e. in a book*
entitled	*e. to it; e. to go*
excited	*e. about/at it*
faced	*f. with it*
inclined	*i. to go*
interested	*i. in it; i. to hear it* (see **interested**)
known	*k. to the police; k. to go there*
married	*m. to her* (see **marry**)
obliged	*o. to you* (= grateful); *o. to go* (= compelled)
occupied	*o. in agriculture*
persuaded	*p. of the truth; p. that it's true*

pleased	*p. with you/a present; p. at/about the news; p. to hear it; p. that he came*
prepared	*p. for it; p. to do it*
puzzled	*p. at/about it; p. that he came; p. why he came*
related	*r. to you/it*
relieved	*r. at the news; r. to hear it; r. that he's safe*
satisfied	*s. with you/it; s. that it's true*
scared	*s. of snakes; s. to go; s. that he might fall*
shocked	*s. at you/it; s. to hear it; s. that he failed*
surprised	*s. at you/it; s. to hear it; s. that he came*
terrified	*t. of dogs; t. at the thought; t. to go; t. that he might fall*
tired	*t. of it*

(See also **word and preposition**; and *The BBI Combinatory Dictionary of English* by Benson, Benson and Ilson: John Benjamins, 1986.)

2. Although these are not true passives, they are not quite ordinary adjectives either. Most English adjectives can be made stronger by combining them with *very*. There is no problem with the most 'adjective-like' ones. You can say *I was very tired* or *very pleased*, just as you say *very happy* or *very cold*. But when these words seem closer to the verb from which they are formed, we usually use *much* or *very much*: *I'm (very) much obliged to you; her English is (very) much improved.*

Sometimes another adverb is more suitable: *badly injured; greatly exaggerated; deeply embarrassed* (see **intensifiers**). In the list above, all except *obliged* either accept *very* or are not gradable.

very see **too**

veteran see **false friends**

video see **television**

view see **scenery**

visit see **sightseeing**

voyage see **journey**

wake/waken see awake

want

1. | TYPICAL MISTAKES: *He wanted (that) we should leave. *She wants I lend her the car.

You should say: *He wanted us to leave. She wants me to lend her the car.*

2. want/need

We *need* things that are necessary. We may *want* (= wish for) unnecessary things that it would be nice to have: *Children need milk. What do you want for your birthday?* Often we 'wish for' necessary things, and then we use either word: *Will you be wanting/needing the car today?* We use either word about things that ought to be done: *The soup needs/wants more salt.*
    You want is often used when giving advice: *You want to bandage that ankle.*

warnings

Here are some useful phrases to use when warning people. The expressions with *mind* are esp. BrE:

'Think about what you are doing.'

> *Be careful! Careful! Mind! Mind out! Watch out! (Be) careful of/with those plates! Mind my glasses! (Be) careful/Mind you don't slip! (Be) careful/Mind/Watch how you open it! Mind/Watch where you put your feet! Hold it!* (= stop. Don't move.)

'You are in danger.'

> *Mind the step! Look out! Watch out—there's a car coming! Watch out for the dog! Hold tight!* (= cling onto something)

water (verb)

| TYPICAL MISTAKE: *My nose is watering.

Eyes *water*, perhaps from smoke, and mouths *water* at the sight of food; but you must say *My nose is running.*

way

1. way/route/road, etc.

Way and *route* both mean a line or direction of travel between places: *Is this the way to the station? You're going the wrong way.* A complicated, or fixed, line of travel is a *route: transatlantic air routes.*

We do not use either of these words when speaking of a particular road, street, lane, etc.: *children playing in the street; driving along country lanes* (see **street(1)**).

2. on/in the way

> TYPICAL MISTAKE: **I can't get through – there's a lorry on the way.*

If something prevents you from moving freely, it is *in the way* or *in your way: There's a lorry in the/my way.* On the way or *on your way* means 'during a journey': *We stopped for lunch on our way to Brighton.*
(For *Do it (in) this way*, see **¹like(3).**)

wear see carry

wedding see marry

weep/cry

> TYPICAL MISTAKE: **I can hear the baby weeping.*

Weep is a formal, literary word, and it implies tears and sorrow rather than noise. If you can *hear* the baby, then it is *crying.*

well see sick(3)

well-known see famous

what

1. What . . .?/How . . .?
(a)

> TYPICAL MISTAKES: **What does it taste/smell/sound/feel/look? *How does it taste/smell/sound/feel/look like?*

What here is a pronoun, and pronouns 'stand for' nouns. The answers to these *what*-questions could not be **It tastes onions* (= noun). You would have to answer *It* *tastes like* (or *of*) *onions*. So we need *like*. The questions should be: *What does it taste/smell/sound/feel/look like?*

How here is an adverb, used for asking about the way of doing something, or the way in which somebody or something behaves (see **[1]like(3)**). The answer to such a *how*-question could not be **It tastes like horrible*, so we do not use *like* thus (though in nonstandard spoken English we find *it tastes, like* (= sort of), *horrible*). The questions should be: *How does it taste/smell/sound/feel/look?*

(b)

> TYPICAL MISTAKE: **How do your friends call you?*

Here we need the pronoun *what*, because the answer will be a noun: *'What do your friends call you?' 'They call me Pip.'* But we could ask: *'How do your friends find your house?' 'I've drawn a map.'*

(c) Sometimes we can use these *what*-questions and *how*-questions with the same meaning: *How was the food?* = *What was the food like?* (For *How do you do?* see **greetings**.)

2. Compare:

> *I don't know what to say. I don't know what I'll say.*
> *I don't know where to go. I don't know where I'll go.*

When these '*wh*-words' (*what, where, who, when,* etc. are used with a *to*- infinitive, they mean *I don't know what I ought to say*, etc. When they are used with a clause, as in the right-hand sentences, they mean *I haven't yet decided what I'm going to say*, etc. Another person can *tell you* (= advise you) *what to say*, or they can *tell you* (= predict) *where you'll go*. (For the choice between *what* and *which*, see **which.**)

when

1. when/as/while

All these words are used about time. Use *as* to show that two gradual things happen at the same time, and are connected: *As the employees retire, they are replaced.* Use *when* to show what happened first: *They left when I arrived* (= a moment afterwards). Use *when* to show that something happened suddenly, in the middle of a state that was going on at the time: *I was alone when the bomb exploded.* Or express the same idea the other way round, with *while: The bomb exploded while I was alone. While* also means that two things were going on together: *While she was abroad I was studying at home.*

Both *as* and *when* can express the idea of 'cause'. Use *as* if one gradual change depends on another. Use *when* if a gradual change causes an event. Compare:

> *As the weather grew colder, we wore thicker and thicker clothes.*
> *When the weather grew colder, we drained the swimming-pool.*

Use *when* if one event causes another: *He was furious when I told him.*

2. | TYPICAL MISTAKE: *We bought the house on the day as Tracy was born.* |

When can introduce an adjectival clause, but *as* cannot unless preceded by a correlative word (esp. *as, same, such, so*) (see **relative clauses**). You must say: *We bought the house on the day when/that/(formal) on which Tracy was born*, or *We bought the house the day Tracy was born*, or *We bought the house (on) the same day (as/that) Tracy was born.*

3. | TYPICAL MISTAKE: *She fell asleep as watching TV.* |

You must say: *She fell asleep as she was watching TV*, or *She fell asleep when watching TV. When*, and some but not all other conjunctions, can introduce an 'abbreviated' clause. It is perfectly correct to leave out *she was* after *when* but not after *as*.

whether

| TYPICAL MISTAKE: *If he comes or not, I'll go.* |

You must say: *Whether he comes or not, I'll go.* Both *whether* and *if* can be used, with the same meaning, in sentences like this: *Do you know whether/if the letters have come?* But we use *whether*, not *if*:

(a) when it introduces the subject of the sentence: *Whether he comes doesn't matter.*
(b) before a *to*- infinitive: *I don't know whether to go.*
(c) after prepositions: *It all depends on whether he comes.*
(d) after nouns: *It's his decision whether he comes or stays away.*
(e) before *or not*; or with the meaning 'whatever happens': *I'll go, whether he comes or not/whether or not he comes.*

which

1. which/what

Use *which* in questions where there is a known list of possibilities, *what* when choosing from an unknown number. Compare:

> *Which did you buy, daffodils or tulips?*
> *What did you buy?*

Note the phrase *What of it?* (= what difference does it make?) (For the choice between *which* and *who*, see **who(1)**.)

2. which/that

> TYPICAL MISTAKE: *the speed at that he drives.*

You must use *which*, not *that*, after a preposition: *the speed at which he drives.*

3. and which, etc.

> TYPICAL PROBLEM: *?These rebels were reacting to something already a quarter of a century old, but of which most people have become aware only in the last decade.* (Alistair Cooke)

It is considered incorrect in English to write *and which, but who,* or *that* in a sentence which does not already contain an earlier *which, who, whom, whose,* or *that.* The author should have written: *These rebels were reacting to something which was already a quarter of a century old, but of which . . .*

while see awhile; when

who

1. who/which/that

(a)

> TYPICAL MISTAKE: *hospitals who haven't enough money.*

In relative clauses, use *who* or *that* for people; *which* or *that* for things; *that* for a mixture of people and things. Compare:

> *hospitals which/that haven't enough money*
> *the girl who/that won the prize*
> *children and animals that play together* (See **that(1)**.)

We sometimes use *who* about a pet animal, and sometimes *which* about a baby. (See **he or she(2)**.)

(For the choice between *who, which* and *that* with reference to human groups, see **singular or plural?(1)**.)

(b)

> TYPICAL MISTAKE: *Who of you is the best swimmer?*

In questions, use *Which of . . .?* even about people. *Who* and *what* are never followed by *of*: *Which of you is* (or *Who is*) *the best swimmer?* (See **which(1)**.) But *Who among you is the best?* is all right, if formal.

2. who's/whose

> TYPICAL MISTAKE: *Who's is this coat?

Who's means either 'who is' or 'who has'. *Whose* means 'of whom?' or 'of which'.
Compare:

> *Who's* (= who is) *coming?*
> *Who's* (= who has) *taken it?*
> *Whose is this coat? Whose coat is this?*

(For *and who*, see **which(3)**. See also **what(2); it's(1)**.)

whole see all

wholesome see healthy

win

1. win/beat/defeat

> TYPICAL MISTAKE: *She won me at darts.

You *win* games, wars, or prizes. You *beat* people in games, or *defeat* them in wars:

> *She won a game of darts (against me).*
> *She beat me (at darts).*
> *William I won the battle of Hastings in 1066.*
> *He defeated the Saxons.*

2. win/earn/gain

> TYPICAL MISTAKE: *How does Gilbert win his living?

When you are paid money for work, you *earn* it: *How does he earn his living? He's earning £300 a week.*

If you *earn* something, it means that you deserve it, even if you don't get it: *She works so hard that she's earned a rest.* If you *gain* something (not money), you get it, even if you don't deserve it: *to gain experience/attention/confidence.* You can use any of these words to express the idea of deserved success: *He won/gained/earned universal admiration.*

wish

1.

> TYPICAL MISTAKE: *I wish we would have a dog.

Clauses after *wish* are formed with the subjunctive, or just with a non-present indicative. You must say: *I wish we had a dog. I wish I were/was rich.*

You can use *would* after *wish* only when it means 'be willing': *I wish you would listen to me.* (See **subjunctive(3)**.)

2. wish/hope

We use both these words about good things. *Wish* is for impossible or unlikely things that we want: *I wish you had told me* (= but you didn't). *Hope* is for good things that will probably happen or are probably true: *I hope you enjoyed yourself.*

(For the choice between *I hope it snows* and *I hope he'll help*, see **future tense(3)**.)

with/in/on

All these words can be used about various abstract circumstances and conditions, and are often confused. (For *in/on* with times and places, see **at/in/on**.)

1. | TYPICAL MISTAKE: **I wrote it with pencil.*

We usually use *in* for a method of writing, or a medium of expression. We use *with* for a tool or instrument, or anything used for a purpose (see **by(1)**). Do not mix them:

> *I wrote it in pencil/in ink/in biro* (but *by hand/on a typewriter*).
> *I wrote it with a pencil/with a pen/with a biro.*
> *a letter in French; talking in whispers*
> *eat it with a spoon*

2. These more abstract meanings of *with/in/on* are often connected with their more literal meanings, which may help you to guess which one to use.

(a) Use *with* for the idea of 'having, possessing, accompanying': *a boy with red hair; I read it with interest.*
(b) Use *in* for the idea of 'included, contained': *too much salt in the soup; a character in a novel; a knight in armour* (always *in* for clothes).
(c) Use *on* for something that 'supports' something else or makes it work: *to live on fish; The car runs on petrol; I bought it on credit.*
(d) Other usages must be learnt. Compare the examples set out below.

with = because of	**in** = because of	**on** = because of
blue with cold; trembling with rage; screaming with laughter; wet with rain (but *suffering from/?with diabetes*)	*stare in surprise*	

with = state, condition	**in** = state, condition	**on** = state, condition
	in public; in secret; in love; in confidence; in danger; in difficulties; in a bad temper; in a hurry; in doubt; in tears; in ruins; in the rain; in the night (see **night***); in search of gold*	*on fire; on holiday; on sale (or for sale); on purpose; on principle; on the alert (for in/on the way, see* **way(2)***)*
with = as regards, about	**in** = as regards, about	**on** = as regards, about
trade with China; in love with Lucy; level with the floor; what's wrong with the car?	*blind in one eye; a degree in engineering; equal in distance; 10 m in length; her interest in music*	*a tax on petrol; an improvement on last year; a lecture on hydrocarbons (see* **about(2)***)*
with = activity	**in** = activity	**on** = activity
	in business; in politics; a job in insurance/in a bank	*a job on a newspaper; serve on a committee; which side are you on?*
with = 'being a'	**in** = 'being a'	**on** = 'being a'
	in return; in exchange; in answer to your letter	

(See also **verbal adjectives; word and preposition**.)

woman

1. woman/lady/girl

An adult female is a *woman*. *Lady* is a polite word, used perhaps about a very old woman, or when speaking of a woman in her presence (*please bring this lady some coffee*). *Ladies and gentlemen* is used when addressing a mixed group. Use *woman* before another noun (*a woman doctor, women students*). You can call a female child or a young woman a *girl*. Old-fashioned women may call their circle of female friends *the girls*, but modern feminists do not care for this. Do not call a girl a *youth*, because that means a boy or a young man.

In theory, *woman* corresponds to *man*, *girl* to *boy*, and *lady* to *gentleman*; but in fact *lady* is probably used more widely than *gentleman*, both for reasons of euphemism and because the word has been taken up by feminists, particularly with 'evaluative' adjectives, as in *She's a very talented lady*.

2. | TYPICAL MISTAKES: **Please introduce me to John's woman.* |

If she is married to John, she is his *wife*. Do not call her his *woman* unless she is his mistress and you want to be rude. Be careful! (See also **man**.)

word and preposition

Verbs, nouns and adjectives may all present us with the problem of which preposition should follow them, so we show here some common ones. We include for completeness some other common patterns (*careful to lock it, complain that it's cold*). Note that the pattern is often the same for a word whether it is a verb or a noun: we say *He knocked* (verb) *at the door* and *I heard a knock* (noun) *at the door*; but sometimes the pattern is different: we say *I hope* (verb) *to go* and *I hope it's true*, but *There's no hope* (noun) *of success*. In the list below, we give derivatives only when their prepositions are different. (See also **verbal adjectives; verb patterns**; and *The BBI Combinatory Dictionary of English* by Benson, Benson and Ilson: John Benjamins, 1986.)

accuse	*a. you of murder*
afraid	*a. of you/it; a. to go; a. that he'll fail*
aim	*a. at it; a. to succeed*
angry	*a. with you; a. at it* (see **angry**)
anxious	*a. about you/it; a. to know; a. that they should know*
apply	*a. to you for a job*
aware	*a. of it; a. that it's true*
bad	*b. at Latin; b. for you*
believe	*b. in it* (see **believe**); *b. that he's Swiss*
blame	*b. you for it; b. it on you*
boast	*b. of /about it*
bored	*b. by/with you/it*
careful	*c. with/of it; c. to lock it; c. that you don't fall*
chance	*c. of it; c. to do it; c. that he'll come* (see **chance(1)**)
complain	*c. of/about it; c. that it's cold*
conceive	*c. of it*
confess	*c. to it; c. that he did it*
congratulate	*c. you on it*
consist	*c. of/in it* (see **comprise**)
convenient	*c. for you*
cure	*c. you of headaches*
decide	*d. on it; d. to go; d. that I'm wrong; d. which to buy*
depend	*d. on you/it; d. where you live*
dependent	*d. on you/it; d. on where you live*
deprive	*d. you of it*
desire	*d. for it; d. to win; d. that he should marry* (see **desire**)
determine	*d. on it; d. to do it; d. that we'll go; d. what to do*
die	*d. of hunger*
different	*d. from you/it* (see **different(1)**)
dispose	*d. of it*
divide	*d. 6 by 3; d. 3 into 6*
doubt (noun)	*d. about/of it; d. if/whether it's true*
dream	*d. about/of it; d. that I'm flying*
example	*e. of it; e. to you*

fail	*f. in Latin; f. to come*
fed up	*f.u. with you/it*
fond	*f. of you/it*
fondness	*f. for you/it*
friendly	*f. with/to/towards you* (see **friendly**)
full	*f. of it*
good	*g. at sums; g. for you*
grateful	*g. to you; g. for it*
guard	*g. against it*
guilty	*g. of murder*
hear	*h. of/about it; h. that she's failed* (see **hear(2)**)
hope (verb)	*h. to go; h. that it's true*
hope (noun)	*h. of success*
independent	*i. of you/it*
indifferent	*i. to it*
indignant	*i. at/over/about it*
inferior	*i. to it*
information	*i. about/on it*
innocent	*i. of the crime*
insist	*i. on it; i. that it's true*
jealous	*j. of you*
kind	*k. to you*
knock	*k. at/on the door*
liable	*l. to headaches; l. to cry*
listen	*l. to you/it* (see **hear(1)**)
look	*l. at/for it* (see **look(1)**)
member	*m. of it*
membership	*m. of it* (BrE)/*in it* (AmE)
nervous	*n. about/of it*
nice	*n. to you*
point (verb)	*p. to/at it*
prefer	*p. cats to dogs* (see **prefer(1)**)
pride	*p. in you/it; p. in admitting it; p. that he's won*
proud	*p. of you/it; p. to admit it; p. that he's won*
repent	*r. of it*
sick	*s. of it*
similar	*s. to it*
succeed	*s. in it*
superior	*s. to it*
sure	*s. of it; s. to win; s. that she'll win*
suspect (verb)	*s. you of murder*
talk	*t. to you; t. about you/it*
think	*t. about/of it; t. that it's true* (see **think**)
translate	*t. it into/from Greek*
warn	*w. you of/about it*
worry	*w. about/over it; w. that he may fail*

Note: Some very common verbs form too many possible combinations to be listed here.

> TYPICAL MISTAKE: **I can't do anything against it.*

You must say *I can't do anything about it.* For a verb such as *do*, consult your dictionary, looking carefully at the examples.

word order

1. adjuncts and other adverbials and adverbs

> TYPICAL MISTAKE: **She married soon/on Friday/last week a millionaire.*

These adverbs and adjuncts do not come between verb and object in an English sentence. There are three places where they can come:

(a) at the beginning: *Soon she married a millionaire.*
(b) in the middle, between subject and verb: *She soon married a millionaire.* (Here, the adverb follows an auxiliary verb, or an auxiliary if there is more than one: *She has already married a millionaire.*)
(c) at the end or after the verb: *She married a millionaire in 1989.*

It often does not matter where you put an adjunct. You can say *I recently met her in Rome* or *I met her in Rome recently* or *I met her recently in Rome.* This is particularly true where there is no object, but there may be a slight change of emphasis. Compare:

> *We went to the zoo on our bikes* (= that is how we travelled).
> *We went on our bikes to the zoo* (= that is where we went).

The general rules are:

(a) Single-word adverbs can come in the middle position, but not usually phrases. We cannot say **I in Rome met her recently.* Phrases usually come at the end, but occasionally at the beginning, as with *before breakfast* below:

> *He read the newspaper before breakfast.*
> *Before breakfast he read the newspaper.*

But if the object is very long, and the adjunct itself is long, the adjunct can sometimes come between verb and object: *He read before breakfast a newspaper account of the impending war.*
(b) Where there are several adjuncts, they are usually arranged in the order place + time + manner, or place + manner + time:

> *Run home* (= place) *quickly* (= manner), *children.*
> *She's been digging in the flowerbed* (= place) *all morning* (= time).
> *She goes home* (= place) *every day* (= time) *by bus* (= manner).
> *She goes home* (= place) *by bus* (= manner) *every day* (= time).

(c)

> TYPICAL MISTAKE: *Always she asks the same questions.*

Always, barely, ever, hardly, never, rarely, scarcely and *seldom* come in the middle position:

> *She always asks the same questions.*
> *She doesn't ever ask the same questions.*

(d) In formal writing *even*, *also* and *too* should be placed to emphasize the word or words they refer to. Compare:

> *Even Simon* (= so certainly everyone else) *worked at Christmas.*
> *Simon worked even at Christmas* (= so certainly on ordinary days).

But in speech, the second *even* usually comes between the subject and the verb, and *also* and *too* come at the end: *Simon even worked at Christmas.* (See **also; only(1)**.)
(e) Be careful that an adverb goes with the right part of the sentence. Compare:

> *Particularly small children find this difficult* (= children who are particularly small).
> *Small children, particularly, find this difficult* (= more than other people. See also **specially(2)**).
> *Small children find this particularly difficult* (= more than usually difficult).

Perhaps and *probably* are 'sentence adverbs', applying to the sentence as a whole. You can say *Probably he won't tell her* or *He probably won't tell her*, but not **He won't probably tell her.*

2. phrasal verbs of the form verb + adverb

Transitive phrasal verbs like *put on* and *throw away* can be used in two possible word orders with an object: *Put your socks on* = *Put on your socks.* If the object is a short pronoun, only one order is possible: *Put them on. Throw it away.* But if the object is very long use the other order: *Put on those lovely red socks that your mum knitted.*

3. ditransitive verbs

(See **verb patterns(6)**.)

(a) *Give her my love* is probably a better word order than *Give my love to her*, but it depends on the length of the two objects. A short pronoun object usually comes first, particularly if it is the direct object:

> *Give it to Sam* (not **Give Sam it.*)
> *Give everything to Sam* or *Give Sam everything.*

With two short pronouns, we usually say: *Buy them some* (rather than *Buy some for them*). With two nouns, you can choose: *Give Mrs Tyson my love* = *Give my love to Mrs Tyson.*

(b) You can use the verb + indirect object + direct object pattern only if you are talking about people. Compare:

> *Make a sweater for him = Make him a sweater.*
> *Make a shelf for the books* (but not **Make the books a shelf*).

But for the pattern *give it a wash*, see **verb or noun?(3)**.

4. *-ed* participles

> TYPICAL MISTAKE: **all the involved people.*

The most 'adjective-like' of these *-ed* participles (see **verbal adjectives**) can be used before a noun: *the tired children; her delighted parents.* The others retain their verbal quality, and are placed after the noun. We say *all the people involved*, which is short for *the people who are involved.*

5. 'a nice cup of tea'

When we speak of a set or group or amount *of* something (see **piece**), we can often attach an adjective to either of the words: *an expensive set of tools = a set of expensive tools.* Sometimes, usage dictates one word order rather than another: *a piece of good advice* (rather than *a good piece of . . .*). At other times, you must consider what makes sense. We must obviously say *a big lump of lead*, not **a lump of big lead.*

6. split infinitive

> TYPICAL PROBLEM: *? 'to slowly trace the forest's shady scene'* (Lord Byron)

This is a split infinitive. The adverb *slowly* comes in between the parts of the *to*-infinitive *to trace.* Good writers have been doing this for many centuries (Byron was a great poet) but it has come to be considered bad English, so avoid it if you can. You could say *slowly to trace*, or *to trace it slowly.*

Sometimes we cannot avoid splitting. In a sentence like *We expect costs to more than double*, there is nowhere else to put *more than.* In *They advised me to kindly ignore the matter*, *kindly* goes with *ignore*; but if we say *They advised me kindly to ignore it*, *kindly* goes with *advised*, which means something quite different.

work/job/employment, etc.

> TYPICAL MISTAKES: **She's got a research work at Oxford/an employment in a bank.*

Work and (more formal) *employment* are uncountable nouns when they mean what you do to earn your living. The common countable noun with the same meaning is *job: She's got a research job/a job in a bank.*

Sometimes you can use either *work* or *job*: *Cleaning the sewers is a dirty job/is dirty work*. But compare:

Please state your occupation (= what work you do) *on the form.*
The factory closed, with a loss of 500 jobs.
It used to provide a lot of employment locally.

Post and *position* are more formal words for a specified job: *a post/position as assistant cashier in a bank*.

A *work* (countable) is something produced, particularly in the arts: *the works of Shakespeare*. *Work* can also mean the place where you work: *She left her tennis racket at work*. More formally, this is your *workplace* or *place of work*.

If you are unemployed and looking for a job, you are *out of work*. Do not use that expression if you simply do not work, perhaps because you are retired or a housewife. You might say *I haven't got a (paid) job*.

To ask a stranger what his or her job is, say *What do you do?*

wound see hurt

wrong(ly) see adjective or adverb?(4)